ADVENTURES IN TRANQUILLITY

ADVENTURES IN TRANQUILLITY

*AN INTRODUCTORY ESSAY
AND AN ANTHOLOGY*

By A. and E. Matson

PHILOSOPHICAL LIBRARY
New York

*"To know the universe itself as a road, as many
roads, as roads for travelling souls."*

WALT WHITMAN

TABLE OF CONTENTS

ACKNOWLEDGMENTS

Acknowledgments are here made to the following publishers and authors who have through their courtesy or by special arrangement or by both permitted the reprinting of certain enumerated passages on which they hold copyright. Pains have been taken to find the proper holders of these and in case any selections have been overlooked or wrongly attributed sincere apologies are offered.

To Houghton Mifflin Company thanks are due for words from the work of Ralph Waldo Emerson, of James Russell Lowell, of Henry David Thoreau and of John Burroughs. Also by special arrangement for the poem "Pandora's Song" by William Vaughan Moody, quoted by the permission of Houghton Mifflin Company.

To Charles Scribner's Sons for the poem "Courage" reprinted from "Moods, Songs and Doggerels" by John Galsworthy; copyright 1912 by Charles Scribner's Sons, 1940 by Ada Galsworthy; used by permission of the publishers.

And for "To The Modern Man" reprinted from "The Beloved Adventure" by John Hall Wheelock; copyright 1912 by Sherman French & Co., 1917 by John Hall Wheelock; used by permission of the author.

Also for the lines from "The Splendid Spur" by Arthur Quiller-Couch.

To the Macmillan Company for the poem "Three Counsellors" by A. E., from his "Selected Poems" published 1935 by the Macmillan Company and used by special arrangement with the permission of the publisher.

To Little Brown & Company for the lines from Emily Dickinson from her "Poems" edited by Martha Dickinson Bianchi and Alfred Leete Hampson, published by Little Brown & Company 1937, copyright 1929 by Martha Dickinson Bianchi.

To Rinehart and Company Inc., for "Miracle", copyright by Lizette Woodworth Reese, reprinted by permission of the publishers.

To the Christian Science Publishing Society for the following poems: "These Things Shall Teach" by Maude D. Newton; "First Green of Spring" by Elizabeth Coatsworth; "When Thought Lies Beautiful And Kind" by Eleanor Baldwin.

ADVENTURES IN TRANQUILLITY

To Liveright Publishing Corporation for the poem "He Whom A Dream Hath Possessed" by Shaumas O'Sheel.

To Harper and Brothers for "Certainty" from "Selected Poems" by John Oxenham by Charles Wallis, Editor, copyright by Erica Oxenham 1948 and used by permission of Harper and Brothers.

To Longmans Green & Co., Inc. for their courtesy in regard to the lines "The Things I Miss" by Thomas Wentworth Higginson.

To Harcourt Brace and Company for the poem "Faith" from "Selected Poems and Parodies of Louis Untermeyer", copyright 1935 and used with the permission of the poet and the publisher.

Also I wish to thank the authors who have kindly given me their individual permissions, Mrs. Elizabeth Coatsworth Beston, Miss Yetza Gillespie, Professor David Morton, Mr. Louis Untermeyer, and (for use of the poem by the late Eleanor Baldwin), to thank her mother, Mrs. Josephine L. Baldwin.

I.
INTRODUCTORY ESSAY: CREATIVE CHEERFULNESS

INTRODUCTORY ESSAY:
CREATIVE CHEERFULNESS

STRANGE, TO THINK THAT most men after they have matured find cheerfulness no longer a mere matter of course, but rather a matter of creativity. Even Dr. Albert Schweitzer has admitted that his "knowledge is pessimistic" but his "willing and hoping . . . optimistic."

As our years increase that "willing and hoping" become more and more important. We know that in spite of the clamor and multitudinousness of the things around us making for misery and distrust there is, after all, a "burning bush and a still small voice" hinting of other things. We know too that those—the inner realities—make for goodness and gladness. And we may discover that through the ages there have been certain men of wisdom and power so alert to those realities that they could even catch and fashion them into an Art, the art of cheerfulness.

The following pages are an attempt to rediscover and re-evaluate a moiety of their happy wisdom.

FIRST, OF HAPPINESS AND HABIT

"Powerful indeed is the empire of habit."

PUBLIUS SYRUS

THESE TWO WORDS may not seem to go together. But
think a moment. I, for my part, remember how when I
was a child I was deeply impressed by two grandparents
of totally opposite types. One was always looking on the
dark side of things, was indeed a slave to the demon
Worry.

> "Trouble, trouble, all around,
>   Ever weighed her to the ground;
>   When the trouble couldn't be seen,
>   'Twas the other side of the bridge I ween."

The other grandparent was a philosopher who had
made happiness, or at least, cheerfulness, a habit. She,
perhaps, may have been blessed with a predisposition
toward happiness, but whether that was so or not, she
had undoubtedly cultivated the trait so successfully that
she had made it into a veritable art.

She lived in an environment which most of us today
would have pronounced asphyxiating, but instead of
complaining, she would laugh and say, "Take comfort,
child, take comfort,—right in the midst of Purgatory."
She had an odd phrase for what she did with her worries: she never disowned them but just "transmogrified"
them.

Oliver Wendell Holmes, the witty physician and father of the equally famous and witty Chief Justice, laid
such stress on heredity that he declared to be well-born

5

a man needed to "begin with his great-grandfather." Today we think differently. We recognize that each human being is freighted with burdens and with treasures in the shape of inherited "tendencies" but we stress rather the fact that each ego is given also a Will with which to select from the legacy of the past only what is most suited to him. He may, to be sure, passively accept the accumulated burdens,—but he may will to pass those by and take the treasure trove.

So, whenever I am reminded of those two forebears of mine whose traits stand out so vividly before me, I realize that similarly contradictory traits may be struggling in me. Then do I make especial effort to WILL WELL,—to fortify myself against the Blue Devils, who tormented the first forebear and emulating the second, to emphasize the happinesses in life,—try to make if not haply an art, at least a habit of cheerfulness.

But how? Ay, there's the rub.

First of all, at any rate, I have to acknowledge the importance of every thought I entertain. What I think makes me. Descartes put it neatly: *"I think, therefore I am."* An older thinker, Marcus Aurelius said, "The essence of things is in thy thoughts about them. . . . What is outside thy circle of thought is nothing at all to it; hold to this and you are safe . . ."

Thomas Traherne, one of those seventeenth century poets whom we call "quaint," wrote:

". . . That Temple David did intend
  Was but a Thought, and yet it did transcend
    King Solomon's. A Thought we know
  Is that for which
  God doth enrich
  With Joys even Heaven above, and Earth below."

"Give me a thought," said Richter, "that I may refresh myself." Thank Heaven, say I, for every new point of view. And such new viewpoints I may get, if from no other where else, from the wisdom of master minds of the past as stored up in books. True, we have been warned by Emerson to "read *only*" to start our own train of thoughts. But what a start those Best Books can give us!

And the idea needful to us may come from some new volume, perhaps oftener from an old one.

I particularly relish one forgotten tale about a *Shepherd of Salisbury Plain*. This shepherd descants to a traveller from town, who chances to come by, about how he keeps his "peace of mind." "You must know, Sir," said this natural philosopher, "as I pass the best part of my time alone, 'tis a great point with me to get comfortable matter for my thoughts; so that 'tis rather self-interest in me to allow myself no pleasures and no practices that won't bear thinking on over and over."

Another of the quaint writers, George Herbert, wrote:
"My soul's a shepherd too,
. . . A flock it feeds
Of thoughts and words, and deeds."

Leigh Hunt claimed that he could make for himself "Nests of pleasant thoughts" and Hawthorne declared that to keep one's imagination happy and wholesome "is one of the truest conditions of communion with heaven."

Whether the fairy godmother has granted us the boon of a naturally happy disposition or not, we can, there is no doubt about it, make conscious endeavor to "keep the imagination centred in the right direction"—we can make a habit of hunting out those "pleasant thoughts" and we can will to let those and those alone color our emotions.

7

Happily such a persistence or habit will range us among the "men of good-will" and in Charles Fletcher Dole's words, "Good Will is the mightiest practical force in the universe." We all know what the old saying Practice makes Perfect implies, and we know how desperately our old world needs the practice of kindliness, of "Goodwill to All Men."

Comforting then is it to remember what the psychologists tell us,— that each little individual endeavor helps, that "our smallest thoughts of good carry with them a seed of good which will assuredly bear fruit in due time." Encouraging to repeat those words of Helen Hunt Jackson, "Next best to natural, spontaneous cheeriness, is deliberate, persistent cheeriness, which we can create, can cultivate, and can so foster and cherish that after a few years the world will never suspect it was not a hereditary gift."

Yes, most of us can profit by Jean Ingelow's hint:

". . . Take joy home
And make a place in thy heart for her,
And give her time to grow, and cherish her,
Then will she come, and oft will sing to thee
When thou art working in the furrow."

II.

CHEERFULNESS AND PHILOSOPHY

CHEERFULNESS AND PHILOSOPHY

"Gentleness and cheerfulness, these come before all morality; they are the perfect duties."

R. L. STEVENSON

To KEEP UP HEART,—this is one of the objectives stressed by all philosophies, whether old or new. And yes, to hold mastery over thoughts and emotions toward such an end —it can be done. "It is not impossible," wrote Anna C. Brackett, in a little booklet of the nineties, "to control imagination. It may be hard, but fighting, even if it brings temporary defeat, is better than not fighting, and what seems defeat is often victory, even if we do not count the increased strength which comes from effort of the will."

More than this, Miss Brackett continued (and here what a modern note she struck!) "There can be no work, whatever it may be, that is so exhausting as painful emotion; while on the other hand mercifully, there is no *tonic* so upbuilding and renewing as joy, which sets into active exercise every constructive power of the body, and whose rush is like the leap of the brooks in spring from the strong mountain-tops to the low-lands."

What is that but another way of putting what the philosopher Spinoza declared? "Cheerfulness can never be excessive, because by it the body's power of action is increased...."

The seventeenth century philosopher was positive on this subject. Listen to him: "Nothing but a gloomy and sad superstition forbids enjoyment.... It is the part of

11

a wise man, I say, to refresh and invigorate himself with moderate and pleasant eating and drinking, with sweet scents and the beauty of green plants, with ornament, with music, with sports, with the theater, and with all things of this kind which one man can enjoy without hurting another."

A later philosopher, Jeremy Bentham, said: "Look out for the bright, for the brightest side of things, and keep thy face constantly toward it." William Blake compared happiness to a chariot. In his mystic eyes it is a chariot that has not only wheels but *wings*. In an illuminating letter to his good friend William Hayley, he wrote: "Time flies very fast and very merrily. I sometimes try to be miserable that I may do more work, but find it is a foolish experiment. Happinesses have wings and wheels; miseries are leaden-legged, and their whole employment is to clip the wings and to take off the wheels of our chariots. We determine, therefore, to be happy. . . ."

Synchronizing with such relatively-speaking New Thought, hear certain of the ancient philosophers on our subject. Hear Marcus Aurelius, for one, saying: "Search thou thy heart! Therein is the fountain of good. Do thou but dig, and abundantly the stream shall gush forth." Again his admonition: "LIVE WITH THE GODS." And still again: "Thy breath is part of the all-encircling air, and is one with it. Let thy mind be part, no less, of that Supreme Mind comprehending all things. For verily, to him who is willing to be inspired thereby the Supreme Mind flows through all things and permeates all things as truly as the air exists for him who will but breathe."

Listen to Epictetus, that slave who, because of his spirit, was a freer man than his master. Epictetus taught that the way to serenity is submission to the will of heaven and that tragedy is but the result of letting our-selves be "bewildered by an admiration of externals...."

"The only real thing," this philosopher claimed, "is to study how to rid life of lamentation, and complaint, and ALAS and I AM UNDONE, and misfortune, and failure, and to learn what death, what exile, what a prison, what poison is; that he may be able to say in a prison like Socrates, 'My dear Crito, if it thus pleases the gods, thus let it be....'" The story goes that a man came to con-sult Epictetus as to how to "persuade his brother to fore-bear treating him ill," and that he received this answer: "Philosophy does not promise to procure any outward good for man; otherwise it would include something be-yond its proper theme. For as the material of a carpenter is wood, of a statuary, brass, so, of the art of living, the material is each man's own life."

So much for a few nuggets from some of the ancient philosophers. But in more modern days we can also go-a-digging for words of wisdom about cheerfulness. Emer-son said, "Life consists in having good days." Another man of Concord, Thoreau, said: "It is something to be able to paint a particular picture, or to carve a statue, and so to make a few objects beautiful; but it is far more glorious to carve and paint the very atmosphere and medium through which we look, which morally we can do. To affect the quality of the day, that is the highest of arts...."

It was another robust poet-philosopher who wrote the famous lines:

"I count life just a stuff
To try the soul's strength on, educe the man."

Not many of us today would be ready to agree with

13

Robert Browning in all of his conclusions. But we can surely go along with him when he says:
"Then welcome each rebuff
That turns earth's smoothness rough
Each sting that bids nor sit nor stand but go!"

III.

AGAINST GLOOM . . . SYMPATHY

AGAINST GLOOM ... SYMPATHY

I heard an angel singing,
When the day was springing:
"Mercy, pity, and peace,
Are the world's release!"

WILLIAM BLAKE

"BUT," CRIES THAT PESSIMISTIC FRIEND, "how can anyone be so Pollyannish? How can one always be philosophical? Especially in moments when all the world about one is at sixes and sevens!"

And truly in addition to the earth-shaking events, the broadcasting and televising of which make for accumulative worry, there are every one's own personal problems, sometimes weighty, sometimes petty enough,—but ever crying out to be solved,—casting black shadows,—intercepting all joy. In face of all our exigencies indeed it seems as if to keep cheerful one would need to be a superman.

Yet even, even in the moments of desperation there are certain valiancies of the soul that we can call on for help. These can bring help not unlike the help which first-aid treatments can bring to physical wounds. There is Sympathy, for instance. There is Humor. There is Perspective-mindedness. ... Three valiancies that have special potency.

First of all, Sympathy. Its worth will be felt if we compare it with a number of other human traits, as did an unidentified writer in the following homely but suggestive lines:

"Order, said the law court;
Knowledge, said the School;
Truth, said the wise man;
Pleasure, said the fool.
Love, said the maiden,
Beauty, said the page;
Freedom, said the Dreamer,
Home, said the sage,
Fame, said the soldier,
Equity, the seer.
Spoke my heart, full sadly,
The answer is not here.
Then within my bosom
Softly this I heard;
'Each heart holds the secret;
Kindness is the word.'"

One of the minor Victorians, Leigh Hunt, who is perhaps too often identified as a maker of light verse merely, once wrote out for himself a little prayer or Beatitude in the form of a prose-poem which is touching and still pertinent. Said Hunt, in his *Religion of the Heart*:

1. Blessed be God; blessed be his beneficence, working towards its purposes in the evening.
2. The portion of the globe on which I live is rolling into darkness from the face of the sun.
3. Softly and silently it goes, with whatever swiftness.
4. Soft and silent are the habitual movements of nature;
5. (Loudly and violently as its beneficence may work within small limits and in rare instances.)
6. Let me imitate the serene habit;
   And not take on my limited foresight the privilege of the stormy exception.

18

May I contribute what I can, this evening, to the
peace and happiness of the house in which I live;
Or of the fellow-creatures, anywhere, among whom
I may find myself.

Kindness, fellow-feeling, sympathy,—how can we keep
these for the Other man when there are so many occasions for friction between us? So many opportunities for
differences of opinion, racial, religious, political, national,
and so many more that can harden into prejudices! And
the prejudices, like stone walls, inexorably shut us out
from each other.

Some rare men have been strong enough to break
down the walls. These "men of the understanding heart"
have learned to look with patience on the faults and
foibles that irritate and anger the rest of us,—have
learned to "make allowances." Even if we cannot understand, to make allowances! That seems asking too much.
But according to a thinker of our own day, Dr.
Schweitzer, "The only bricks of the house of mankind are
the forebearing hearts of innumerable separate persons. . . ."

Strange that we average persons are so slow to see that
such a hard way is the only way. Strange that even when
we finally do see we cannot bring ourselves to be realistic
and practical enough to work out our differences in a
generous spirit of give and take. We do just this in some
of our activities,—in the realm of Sports, for instance.
Why should we not in all our contacts?

There are plenty of old adages to remind us that we
should, and one modern has given a whimsical twist to a
Biblical precept, saying: "Do unto others as if you were
the others." If only we could apply our theories to our
particular problems, whether personal or global!

Then there is another first-aid against low spirits in the cultivation of sympathy with nature, especially with all the small and kindlier aspects of the world we live in. Thoreau said, "Man needs not only to be spiritualized but to be *naturalized* on the soil of earth." Francis of Assisi, we know, would talk not only with birds and little fishes, but even with beasts, to an end of mutual satisfaction. True enough, our age, with its horrific exploitation of the material world, does not lend itself easily to the kinship with nature which Wordsworth and many of the greatest poets have lauded, yet just that might be the greatest help toward the recovery of our equanimity. "The doctrines of despair," to quote Thoreau once more, "of spiritual or political tyranny or servitude were never taught by such as shared the serenity of nature."

The trouble is, man has grown too ambitious. "Stretching out his hand to catch the stars," said old Jeremy Bentham, "he forgets the flowers at his feet." John Burroughs decided that "A man must invest himself near at hand and in common things, and be content with a steady and moderate return, if he would know the blessedness of a cheerful heart, and the sweetness of a walk over the round earth."

Even the common "creature comforts" have their own value in this plight of ours, especially if shared. Dean Sydney Smith was canny as well as witty, and he declared, "I once gave a lady two and twenty recipes against melancholy. . . . One was a bright fire, another to remember all the pleasant things said to her, another to keep a box of sugar plums on the chimney-piece; and a kettle simmering on the hob. . . ."

Which sounds quaint—but only think how suggestive the idea!

Certainly we should not scorn the common joys. We have, yes, "an inalienable right" to them so long as they can be had without harm to others. And happily, we are so made that different men relish different kinds of enjoyment. The one thing needful is to be open-minded, to be receptive—in mind and heart—to all the good and ever better influences.

"Open the door; let in the air!
The winds are sweet, and the flowers are fair,
Joy is abroad in the world to-day;
If our door is wide open, it may come this way,
Open the door!
Open the door of the heart; let in
Sympathy sweet for stranger and kin.
It will make the halls of the heart so fair
That angels may enter unaware.
Open the door!"*

* Author unidentified.

IV.

THEN HUMOR

THEN HUMOR

"The humorist laughs and sympathizes by turns."
EDMOND SCHERER

"GO ON, THEN, MERRILY, TO HEAVEN," said old Richard Burton. And yea verily, another potent first-aid against depression is a sense of humor. A help, did I say? Yes, but it is more. It is positively needful if we are to get through this "vale of tears" without being submerged in self-pity and utterly overcome by the multitudinous "ills that flesh is heir to."

And there is no doubt but that humor and sympathy dovetail. An appreciation of the comic, surely does— as Emerson tersely put it—make "a bond of sympathy" between us all, whatever our sorts and conditions. In her story of Ramona, Helen Hunt Jackson pictured for us a señora of the old days managing a vast estate which required supervision of many workers of many different degrees of intelligence and efficiency. Often she would have to rebuke one or other of these workers, and she would do so in good round terms, but at the same time she would bring out before them some comic side of the matter, and all would be kept in good-humor.

Strangely enough, many men noted for their blithe spirits have had to fight against odds to keep those spirits. Samuel Johnson confessed that the black devils were often after him. But he did fight, and he declared that even in some of the darkest moments "cheerfulness would be breaking in." Charles Lamb had surely cause for gloom but he "had something else to do than to regret"

25

and turning to each task that came to his hand, lit it up with his wit and humor so that the dull task would shine like Aladdin's lamp.

The Autocrat of the Breakfast Table said, "The ludicrous has its place in the universe; it is not a human invention, but one of the Divine Ideas, illustrated in the practical jokes of kittens and monkeys long before Aristophanes or Shakespeare." An unidentified modern has pointed out that after all "there are two things about which one should never worry—that which cannot be helped and that which can be." Kate Sanborn happily compared laughter to a "tidal wave." And well did Shakespeare know whereof he spoke when he wrote:

"A merry heart goes all the day
Your sad one tires in a mile-a."

Adelina Patti was once asked how she had contrived to keep her face so young and fresh looking. She answered that whenever she felt a wrinkle coming she "laughed it away." It is said that when Lydia Maria Child grew old she would make a habit of visiting shops where she could find bright things, textiles and pictures to gloat over, and that in her windows at home she kept rainbow-catching prisms hanging.

It used to be claimed that man is the only animal that laughs—a claim hardly substantiated. But at least we can assert that Humor is one of man's most valuable assets. What is more, we know a laugh is a laugh in any language. Fact indeed that ought to be a help to human beings in solving their racial and international problems.

At any rate, as Scherer put it, "The humorist feels the imperfections of reality, and resigns himself to them with good temper, knowing that his own satisfaction is not the rule of things, and that the formula of the universe is

26

necessarily larger than the preferences of a single one of the accidental beings of whom the universe is composed." In Agnes Rapplier's words, if humor "be powerless to mould existence, or even explain it to our satisfaction, it can give us at least some basis for philosophy, some scope for sympathy, and sanity, and endurance."

We all know that a bow-string cannot be stretched too taut. We know, but we often ignore that fact that our nerves, similarly, must not be kept too long at tension,—must have relief. Shakespeare is one of the notables who recognized this fact. Without benefit of our modern psychology, he knew just how to introduce into his plays comic characters and scenes in such a way that they would not only serve as foils to his more serious characters and moments, but would also give his audience needed relief.

Another amusing and old example of such a psychological awareness is given us by—of all persons—the quaint author of *The Saint's Everlasting Rest and the New Whole Duty of Man*! Said Richard Baxter (and this, mind you, in the seventeenth century), "We must have a care not to extend our thoughts immoderately and more than our tempers will bear, even to the best things, and the way to do that is not to put them too much or too long upon the stretch at any one time, but to relax them when there is occasion, and to let them *run out and entertain themselves....*"

The famous French humorist, who was also a physician, declared:

> "One inch of joy surmounts of grief a span
> Because to laugh is proper to the man."

Laughter, Rabelais would have said today, is not merely proper, but "antiseptic," health-provoking.

What makes us laugh? What things, incidents or creatures, human or otherwise, have given us our best humorous moments? To go on a quest for answers to such questions could lead down an interesting trail. (To be sure, what has seemed ludicrous to one generation, seems sometimes not even faintly funny to another—sometimes for better, sometimes for worse. Consider for instance, certain of the primitive puppet-plays. Contrast them with some of the delightful mummery of today. On the other hand, consider the happy frolickings, all in black and white, of the Brownies which a few of us can remember relishing. Contrast them with the lurid antics of today's creatures in the colored strips.)

But, nonetheless, there are classics of humor. There are situations, there are characters, there are never-neverlands that can be recaptured, that can still make us "chortle in our joy." It does one good once in a while, to shut one's eyes and think back to some of the masterpieces of merriment: To hark back, in fancy, to Don Quixote, to Aesop,—to Mother Goose even,—as to Robin Hood among his Merry Men, and to Touchstone in his Forest of Ardennes . . . good to renew acquaintance with such folk as Dickens, as Jane Austen, as Mark Twain and Frank Stockton, conjured up for our delectation.

Surely not without good reason has man's love of fun been put into him. What one of us, indeed, but has known moments when the Worries, big and little, had accumulated until life seemed dull and leaden—a thing not worth dragging about with any longer. When suddenly, from some quarter of the globe—a word, a look— perhaps no less than a peep into some old volume—and a humorous light thrown on all. We have laughed in spite of ourselves. We have forgotten ourselves and our weary minds have been braced as though a fresh sea breeze had blown in on us. And thereupon were we enabled to carry on.

Yes, "Power" *does* "dwell with cheerfulness. Hope *does* put us in a working mood."

And yes again, that old Scotch poet, William Dunbar was right:

> "Who lives merrily, he lives michtily:
> Without Gladness availès no treasure."

V.

AND PERSPECTIVE-MINDEDNESS

AND PERSPECTIVE-MINDEDNESS

"The vague mystery of a beautiful distance leads the mind out of the world, as the most exquisite music does."
P. G. HAMERTON

AN APPRECIATION OF PERSPECTIVE, (a getting into the way of "looking through" and beyond things that are close at hand, a learning to take long views instead of short),—this can be another help toward attaining our goal of serenity.

It was a capital suggestion that when we are beset by a problem, instead of worrying, we might make a "game" of it,—that "cutting out personal feelings" we exercise whatever we can muster of "cool intellect" and in addition that we take a momentary stand at some distance from the problem. We all realize what an important part perspective plays in the so-called Fine Arts. We see the landscape painter, for instance, using it to make his picture more telling. And as he does so, subordinating certain details and emphasizing others, he succeeds in drawing our attention to his central theme. He makes that *stand out* and we find his scene true to life. But what we do not realize is that the layman too might profitably make a study of this law and by its help make his own everyday work more telling, more effective.

We have all heard of the over-conscientious woman who every night thinks over all the things she hasn't done, and of the frustrated man who was afraid his epitaph would be "not he hath done what he could, but he tried to do what he couldn't." If they had only got in the habit of taking the long view of their activities they might have found out that some things were worth the doing but that others were better left undone. But, of course, after such a discovery and a resolve not to worry over what is unnecessary one must have the stamina to stick to one's resolve. "Above all," said Aurelius, "be not diverted from thy course." And again, "Have readiest to thy hand . . . two thoughts: one, that *things* cannot touch the soul; the other, that things are perpetually *changing.* . . ." Epictetus, another of the ancients who looked at life in perspective, said that "all unavoidable evil in the world is only apparent and external," and that "our happiness depends upon our own will which even Zeus cannot break."

But to come back to a less metaphysical plane—what a marvel it is that natural objects *change* in size and even in color as they are looked at now near, now in the middle distance, and now far away. How exciting it is to reflect that they are not, after all, so inflexible as they had seemed to be in their relationships to each other and to ourselves. How provocative, too, the thought that all depends on our particular "station-point."

So there we are back to the power of will again. We can move our "station," our viewpoint and then all is different. The idea is a little dizzifying but in the long run it is hopeful.

True, it will shake our complacency in our individual importance to watch some object—a tractor, perhaps, in a field that is being ploughed into long, straight furrows, become smaller and smaller, until it is a mere speck on the horizon. We feel that to an observer stationed in some remote conning tower we, too, must be reduced to a mere pin prick on the horizon. (It would be a good exercise in tolerance, by the way, if human beings would now and then consider each other perspectively.)

On the other hand, to look through some lovely vista —to come unexpectedly on some stream or river shining at the end of arching trees—to glimpse some rose-window through the aisles of some mediæval cathedral—is to get a lilt and lift of spirit. Beauty is opened up to us but more than that our consciousness of the beautiful is enhanced by a revelation of continuity.

One of the interesting facts about the old Roman houses is the way their sleeping-rooms, however small they might be (and many of them would seem to us mere cells) would often have perspectives painted on their walls of gardened vistas that led the mind out-of-doors. Out-of-doors, figuratively speaking, away from humdrum Worries.

The slightest study of another of the Fine Arts, that of Landscape Architecture, shows how often and how happily the device of perspective was called upon. Sometimes the long view would be achieved by deft arrangements of the garden material itself; sometimes, to an end of sumptuousness, with the addition of ornamental accessories, such as elaborate trellisworks and stone or marble archways. In arriving at his dazzling effects of distance, the designer of the famous gardens of Versailles, Le Notre, never could get enough sculpture and architectural features to satisfy him. The makers of the quieter old English pleasaunces, on the other hand, relied oftener on living shrubs and trees to get their vistas. As for the homely cottage garths, they too revealed a love of vistas in their simple, perhaps rustic, gates overarched with climbing honeysuckle or roses.

But there, most of us cannot possess frescoed rooms

and gardened vistas. We can however have them or their counterparts in our hearts. We can all cultivate perspective-mindedness. We can remind ourselves of what Blake said:

"... In your own bosom you bear your Heaven
And Earth and all you behold; though it appears Without it is Within,
In your Imagination, of which this World of Mortality is but a shadow."

And as we train our thoughts to look beyond our own specks of selves—on and on—we may begin to understand the lines of the poet Arthur Hugh Clough:

"Go with the sun and the stars, and yet evermore in thy spirit
Say to thyself; 'It is good, yet there is better than it
This that I see is not all, and this that I do is but little
Nevertheless it is good, though there is better than it.' "

Truly, when the Gloom shuts in on us like an ocean fog—when neither sympathy, nor humor, nor any consciousness of perspective values can get through to us—when nothing but a sheer, aching sense of failure apprises us that we still exist—even then we might get some comfort from Saint Augustine and the words he spoke so long and long ago:

"Beware of despairing of yourself;
You are commanded to put your trust in God,
Not in yourself."

VI.
PATIENCE, PERSEVERANCE, AND COURAGE

PATIENCE, PERSEVERANCE, AND COURAGE

*"From the lowest depths there is a path to the loft-
iest heights.*

Thomas Carlyle

Our spirits can be "in the depths" for so many different reasons. Sometimes because of untoward circum-
stance, sometimes (and this is especially hard to "snap
out of") because of failure to live up to our ideals, and
again because of sheer, downright fear. And at such
times there seems nothing for it but to go doggedly on, to
strive after patience, and perseverance and courage.

Times there are indeed when if this Demon Discontent
is caused by that unkind jade, Fortune, or by unkind persons, it may be possible to rout it by turning away and by
dwelling on the thought voiced by Matthew Arnold. In
his famous poem *Self-Dependence* Arnold looks up to the
stars and out to the sea and finds that
> "These demand not that the things without them
> Yield them love, amusement, sympathy"

Instead of making such demands
> ". . . . self-poised they live, nor pine with noting
> All the fever of some differing soul.
> In their own tasks all their powers pouring,
> These attain the mighty life you see."

In other times of desperation nothing seems to help,
unless possibly some such forthright prose as that of old
Epictetus. "Why," asked Epictetus, "why do you not
thank the gods that they have made you superior to those

39

events which they have not placed within your control?" "They discharge you," said he further, "from all responsibility for your parents, for your brothers, for your body, possessions, death, life. For what then have they made you responsible? For that which is alone in your power—a right use of things as they appear."

Even more emphatic on this subject was Aurelius whose imperial duties and responsibilities were not at all to his liking and whose sky was only too often darkened with wars abroad and with troubles at home, domestic as well as civil and political. Yet here is his verdict: "In supreme joyousness of soul thou mayest live though all men revile thee." The *humanness* of that verily noblest Roman is brought touchingly close to us when we learn that his *Sayings* were preserved and treasured through the Dark Ages and on into the Elizabethan era, and that old Captain John Smith (he who discovered Virginia) carried a copy of them on his journeys, finding "therein sweet refreshment in his seasons of despondency."

One of the most difficult kinds of despondency to get relief from is ours in the hours when we suffer too keenly a realization of our own shortcomings. In such hours we become aware that Bunyan's *Slough of Despair* is no fancy but a very real place. To hold lofty aspirations, to make great resolves, then to fail to live up to them—to do the wrong thing and to know you have no thing or body to blame except your own dumb self—this is cause enough for desperation, for a "fit of the blues."

But there,

"To mourn a mischief that is past and gone,
    Is the best way to bring fresh mischief on."

No less experienced a man than William Shakespeare spoke those words. They are worthy of being emblazoned on every day of your engagement calendar if you use one. And as a comforting addenda, one might copy out Lamb's words to his friend Lloyd: "Prepare yourself not to expect too much out of yourself."

And there, stern Dante's admonition is even more pointed:

> "One glance,
>
>   And then pass on."

Truly to bypass despondency, to keep patient and persevering, does require a further virtue—strength of character—Courage. Even when we were not struggling against some particular misfortune, some misunderstanding of our motives, or some inferiority complex, even then so many fears lie in wait to beset us, and the fears come in so many guises! It was hard enough to fight the old fears that could be named and faced, "breast-forward." We had indeed begun to think that we could overcome a few of them—that we could achieve "Freedom from Want," "Freedom from Ignorance" and certain other freedoms . . . When along came quite new and nameless terrors . . . Small wonder we are haunted and inhibited.

But there, fear has always been lurking behind our backs—has always been an inhibitor. Fear and despair together are the blackest, most destructive words in our language. Cheer and Courage, on the contrary, are the most colorful and constructive. And cheer (which derives from an old French word for "face") is the most fitting companion for courage (which is from the latin "cor" or heart). To these two, working together, "All things are possible."

To face the difficulties, to put a brave face on them, to bear "cheerfully" helps us to endure adversity—to muster our courage, to "keep up heart," helps us to meet the unknown as an Adventure.

> "Bate not a jot of heart nor hope,
> But steer right onward . . ."

advised William James, referring to none other than Milton's famous twenty-second sonnet. "Courage," thought Barrie, "is a proof of our immortality."

So here we are brought around to those ideas, old-fashioned to be sure, but still pertinent, of hope and faith. We are shown that we must cling to the hope that right will win out—to the faith that there does exist something fairer and more permanent than what our eyes disclose. The French writer Amiel called discouragement "an act of unbelief." Mazzini condemned it as "disenchanted Egotism." Discounting such entirely, Robert Browning

> "Never dreamed though right were worsted,
>   wrong would triumph,
> Held we fall to rise, are baffled to fight
>   better."

Taking the sunset as a symbol a modern poet, Louis Untermeyer, has suggested how little, after all, can depend upon our senses. According to the evidence of our eyes, the sun every night goes down into darkness, but it goes with faith, "trusting itself" to the unknown. We have absolutely no "proof" about its reappearance. And yet. . . . The poignant lines of *Any Sunset* might well bring comfort to all those who face the loss of loved ones, as they can put heart into all those of us who are paralyzed by doubt and fear.

> "Yet, stab at them that will,
> No stab the soul can kill."

Those are the words of valiant Sir Walter Raleigh.

And if they are too solemn to rest on, we may get a

similar but whimsically-expressed encouragement from another gallant old Englishman:

> " 'Fight on, my men,' says Sir Andrew Barton
> I am hurte, but I am not slaine;
> I'll lie me downe and bleed awhile,
> And then I'll rise and fight againe!"

VII.

THE WORTH AND WISDOM OF CHEERFULNESS

THE WORTH AND WISDOM
OF CHEERFULNESS

"The joyousness of a spirit is an index of its power."
NINON TO SAINT EVREMOND

Is IT A MISTAKE to lay so much emphasis on cheerfulness? I think it is not. It does depend, to be sure, on
what we mean by the word. If we mean mere selfish
indulgence and a fatuous ignoring of the predicament of
ourselves and of others, then, yes, we should give over
praising it. But if we mean a harmonious development
of our various faculties as human beings and a practical
recognition of the equal rights of all other men to the
same development—then, no, a thousand times no—we
cannot give it too much praise or ever have too much of
it.

Spinoza, we remember, contended that "joy increases
the body's power" so that all the parts acquire the same
proportion of motion and rest to each other. "Melancholy," on the contrary, he said, actually "lessens the
body's power of action." The philosopher and the drama-
tist Shakespeare agree that "heaviness," depression of
spirit, is "life-harming." And both of them agree with
Aristotle's claim that happiness is a veritable *"Kind of
Energy."*

Epictetus believed the gods intended all men to be
happy. St. John of the Cross, a contemporary of St.
Teresa, declared: "The first of the passions of the soul
and the will is joy." Alexander Pope, in his famous study
of Man, counted happiness the human being's "end and

47

aim." Our early American forebears, too, in spite of their so-much-talked-of Puritanic bias, actually insisted in their Declaration that "the pursuit of Happiness" is one of the *"inalienable rights"* of *"all men."*

True, happiness is not a Thing—it is one of your intangibles. But it is no mere illusion, nor any sentimental vapor. If it had been such, certainly those hard-headed, clear-thinking Old Colonials of ours would have had none of it! It is one of the positive Values and we have a right to strive valiantly for it, whether for our individual selves or for all men as well.

Ay, there's another of the rubs: how to get this happiness for oneself without affecting adversely someone else's chance of getting it. And (if and when some measure of individual ease and well-being is attained) how to keep it from being ruined, or at best, tarnished by the *un*happiness of others! George Eliot, Herbert Spencer and other Meliorists of their day held the theory that no one person can be truly happy so long as so much misery exists in the world. They held that "All mankind must rise together."

But there, we have to remember that a sum is made up of many a unit, that as someone has well said, "Each man counts." We may as well acknowledge too that there is something actually contagious about good-humor. In fact good-humor is so "catching" that if a single individual has it, he will unconsciously impart it to others. It is a truism that no man is a mere cog in a wheel but also, willy or no, an influence. And because this is so, it is not mere selfishness of each one to make cheerfulness an "end and aim."

Amiel called happiness "cumulative" and the beloved Robert Louis declared: "A happy man or woman is a better thing to find than a five pound note. He or she is a radiating focus of good-will; and their entrance into a room is as though another candle had been lighted. We need not care whether they could prove the fifty-seventh proposition; they do a better thing than that, they practically demonstrate the great Theorum of the liveableness of life."

Unluckily the converse is also true. As good-humor can light up a room and a company, so bad-humor can spread havoc and desolation all around. As a matter of fact, even though not itself material it is a force, and a force for destruction, that can affect material things. To turn to the first chapter of a little-read book of the Old Testament, Joel, is to get a picturesque illustration of this. The Children of Israel had fallen into iniquity and were being punished by their Jehovah with all manner of trials and tribulations, until their spirits were broken. They are depicted as utterly demoralized and lacking in all initiative. Moreover, according to the Biblical narrator, "The vine is dried up, and the fig-tree languisheth; the pomegranate-tree, the palm-tree also, and the apple-tree, *even* all the trees of the field, are withered; because joy is withered away from the sons of men."

Never can we be grateful enough to those who have done aught to revive the sons of men. To those who have "lit up candles."

When it is a question of solving the great issues, the majority of us have to exercise patience rather than any outstanding performance, but we can do our bit to encourage every forward step toward their solution, and we can hearten ourselves with the reflection that each and every individual does indeed count. Fostering every slightest good, we can remind ourselves that it is ilka little that makes the mickle.

And as we all know, the resort to humor can help. Certain rare beings have not waited, either for the coming Utopia or for a cessation of their personal troubles, but have made a definite practice of holding the whimsical attitude toward circumstances. Charles Lamb is a case in point. True, he had a talent that was unique for the discovery of the whimsies, but he also had the will power to stress his discoveries and to do so in such piquant and luminous words that they could move not only his friends and contemporaries but also us, his posterity.

We may remind ourselves too that even today, in spite of all the Frankenstein monsters that are continually being prepared to make us dejected and panic-stricken, there do still exist a-many of those whatsoever things are true, and honest, just and pure, things lovely and of good repute, which the apostle admonished us to think on!

It was an idea of the great German thinker, Goethe, that every man ought each day to learn something new, to hear some good music, to read in some worth-while book, to look upon something beautiful, to meditate, and to *make merry*. Merriment was also praised in the ancient Proverbs: "He that is of a merry heart hath a continual feast." "A merry heart doeth good like a medicine." While in Ecclesiastes it is written that "The gladness of the heart is the life of man, and the joyfulness of a man prolongeth his days."

A more modern writer has suggested that one way to win the cheerful disposition is to hold fast the sense of Wonder. And truly if one only stops to consider, how much there is to wonder at in this vast universe of which our own particular earth is such an infinitesimal mite!

For that matter what wonders in the everyday, so-called ordinary phenomena right here about us! How can we ever allow ourselves to grow callous to the "rosy

morn," to the "happy hills," to the "glad indomitable
sea" any more than to the "starry firmament on high"?
Astonishing how positively the mere words indicating
such gracious things can lift the spirits. There is something re-creative even in a bald inventory of the happy
adjectives—glad, gleeful, mirthful, joyous, jocund. No, it
is not strange that Joy (Cheerfulness) has been called
"the Bloom of Love and Wisdom."

Jean Ingelow considered it "A Grace" which may be
said to God—a thought worth pondering—so also is a
thought expressed by Josephine Peabody. In one of her
loveliest lyrics that poet found inspiration in the way the
balsam fir-tree holds not only its leaves all the winter
through, but also its pungency. So too, she realized she,
likewise, must stand up against all cold and grief and
doubt. She vowed to herself that she too would "keep
the fragrant heart."

Which raises another thought—an exhilarating one. In
those moments when a man, be he poet or just every-day
human being, succeeds in keeping the fragrant heart, in
maintaining the cheerful attitude under whatever circumstances, it may be that he will be conscious of a deep
inner satisfaction—even a glow—which is not to be de-
scribed or defined, but which may be like that fervency
which the men of old felt when they offered incense.

Inspired by a painting of the Magi, Richard Trench
wrote some lines which are poignant as they are rele-
vant:

> May the frankincense, in air
> As it climbs, instruct our prayer
> That it ever upward tend,
> Ever struggle to ascend,
> Leaving earth, yet ere it go
> Fragrance rich diffuse below

51

As the myrrh is bitter-sweet
So in us may such things meet,
As unto the mortal taste
Bitter seeming, yet at last
Shall to them who try be known
To have sweetness of their own

Yes, frankincense and myrrh—offerings which the ancient worshippers would bring to the altar—gifts which the wondering Magi found fit to lay before the Babe in the manger—these are not mere dark words, sounding and vain, rather are they lustrous and full of meaning—symbols of spirit offering which each one of us, even we, today, may make.

ANTHOLOGY OF RESTORATIVE THOUGHTS

Tossed on a sea of troubles, Soul, my Soul,
  Thyself do thou control;
And to the weapons of advancing foes
  A stubborn breast oppose:
Undaunted midst the hostile might
Of squadrons burning for the fight.
Thine be no boasting when the victor's crown
  Wins thee deserved renown;
Thine no dejected sorrow, when defeat
  Would urge a base retreat:
Rejoice in joyous things—nor overmuch
  Let grief thy bosom touch
'Midst evil, and still bear in mind
How changeful are the ways of human-kind.

> *Lines on Equanimity*
> ARCHILOCHUS
> Greek poet of the 7th century B. C.
> Translation by William Hay

... Have readiest to thy hand, above all others, these two thoughts: one, that *things* cannot touch the soul; the other, that things are perpetually changing and ceasing to be. Remember how many of these changes thou thyself hast seen! The Universe is change.

... Search thou thy heart! Therein is the fountain of good. Do thou but dig, and abundantly the stream shall gush forth.

Live with the gods.

> MARCUS AURELIUS ANTONINUS
> (121-180 A. D.)
> from *The Meditations*

Men seek retirement in country-houses, on the sea-coast, on the mountains; and you have yourself as much fondness for such places as another. But there is little proof of culture therein; since the privilege is yours of retiring into yourself whensoever you please—into that little farm of one's own mind, where a silence so profound may be enjoyed.

It is in thy power to think as thou wilt: The essence of things is in thy thoughts about them: All is opinion, conception: No man can be hindered by another: What is outside thy circle of thought is nothing at all to it; hold to this, and you are safe: One thing is needful—to live close to the divine genius within thee, and minister thereto worthily.

MARCUS AURELIUS ANTONINUS
(121-180 A. D.)
from *The Meditations*

Neither riches nor health nor fame nor, in short, anything else is in our power except a right use of the semblances of things. This alone is, by nature, not subject to restraint, not subject to hindrance.

The essence of good and evil is a certain disposition of the will.

Go before no man with trembling, but know well that all events are indifferent to thee. For whatever it may be, it shall lie with thee to use it nobly: this no man can prevent.

EPICTETUS—from the *Discourses*

What makes a happy life, dear friend,
If thou would'st briefly learn, attend.
An income left, not earned by toil;
Some acres of a kindly soil;
The pot unfailing on the fire;
No lawsuits; seldom town attire;

Health; strength and grace; a peaceful mind;
Shrewdness with honesty combined;
Plain living; equal friends and free;
Evenings of temperate gaiety;
A wife discreet, yet blithe and bright;
Sound slumber, that lends wings to night.
With all thy heart embrace thy lot,
Wish not for death and fear it not.

> MARTIAL (43 A. D. - c. 104)
> *Epigrams X*
> Translation by Goldwin Smith
> Macmillan, 1894

Would you be free? 'Tis your chief wish you say,
Come on: I'll show thee, friend, the certain way.
If to no feasts abroad thou lov'st to go,
Whilst bounteous God does bread at home bestow;
If thou the goodness of thy clothes dost prize
By thine own use, and not by other's eyes;
If only safe from weathers, thou canst dwell
In a small house, but a convenient shell;
If thou without a sigh, or golden wish,
Canst look upon thy beechen bowl and dish,
If in thy mind such power and greatness be—
The Persian King's a slave compared to thee.

> MARTIAL—Book 2
> Translation by William Cowper

ON A QUIET LIFE

Small fields are mine; a small and guiltless rent
  In both I prize the quiet of content.
  My mind maintains its peace, from feverish dread
Secure, and fear of crimes that sloth has bred.
Others let toilsome camps or curule chairs
Invite, and joys which vain ambition shares.

May I, my lot among the people thrown,
Live to myself, and call my time my own!

Avienus
Roman poet of about 400 A. D.
Translation by C. A. Elton
See W. W. Best Literature, vol. 28

Health is the greatest gift, contentedness the best riches.

From *The Dhammapada*
(A portion of the Buddhist Scriptures)

BALLAD OF GOOD COUNSEL

Flee fro the prees, and dwelle with sothfastnesse
 Suffice unto thy thyng though hit be small;
For hord hath hate and clymbyng tikèlnesse,
 Prees hath envye, and wele blent overal;
Savour no more than thee behove shall
 Werk well thyself, that other folk canst rede,
 And trouthe shall delivre, it is no drede.

Tempest thee noght al croked to redresse
 In trust of hir that turneth as a bal:
Greet reste stant in litel besynesse;
 An eek be war to sporne ageyn an al;
Stryve noght, as doth the crokke with the wal.
 Daunte thyself, that dauntest otheres dede
 And trouthe shall delivre, it is no drede,

That thee is sent, receyve in buxumnesse,
 The wrastling for this worlde axeth a fall.
Her nis non hoom, her nis but wildernesse.
 Forth, pilgrim, forth! beste, out of thy stall,
Know thy contree, look up, thank God of al;
 Hold the hye wey, and lat thy gost thee lede,
 And trouthe shall delivre, it is no drede.

Envoy

Therefore, thou vàche, leve thyn old wrecchednesse
  Unto the world; leve now to be thral;
Cry him mercy, that of his hy goodnesse
  Made thee of noght, and in especial
Draw unto him, and pray in general
  For thee, and eek for other, hevenlich mede;
  And trouthe shall delivre, it is no drede.

GEOFFREY CHAUCER (1340?-1400)

In sickness and in povertie,
  Be glad therein, thank Me for all,
The more thou hast them in plentie,
  The nearer I shall come withal.
Then say: "Lord, keep me nigh to Thee!
  At need, Lord, hear when I call!
Take from me health, prosperitie,
  Rather than let me from thee fall."

From *God's Appeal to Man*
Author unknown: about 1420

Blessed be simple life, withouten dreid;
  Blessed be sober feast in quietie;
Who has enough, of no more has he need,
  Though it be little into quantitie.
Great abundance and blind prosperitie,
  Oftimes mak an ill conclusion;
The sweetest life, therefore, in this countrie,
  Is to live safe, with small possession.

Content from *The Tale of the Upland*
and the *Burgess Mouse*
ROBERT HENRYSON (1430?-1506?)

NO TREASURE WITHOUT GLADNESS

Be merry, men! and tak not sair in mind
  The wavering of this wretched world of sorrow!
To God be humble and to thy friend be kind,

And with thy neighbours gladly lend and borrow:
  His chance to-nicht, it may be thine to-morrow:
Be blithe in heart for any adventure;
  For oft with wise men, 't has been said aforrow,
Without gladness availïs no treasúre.

Mak thee gude cheer of it that God thee sends,
  For warldes wrack but welfare nocht avails.
No gude is thine, save only what thou spends;
  Remanent all thou brookis but with bales.
  Seek to solace when sadness thee assails;
In dolour long thy life may not endure,
  Wherefore of comfort set up all thy sails;
Without gladness availïs no treasúre.

Follow on pity, flee trouble and debate,
  With famous folk aye hold thy company;
Be charitable and humble in thine estate,
  For warldly honour lastës but a cry;
  For trouble on earth tak no melancholy;
Be rich in patience, if thou in goods be poor;
  Who lives merrily he lives michtily;
Without gladness availïs no treasúre.

Thou seest these wretches set with sorrow and care
  To gather goods in all their livés space;
And, when their bags are full, their selves are bare,
  And of their riches but the keeping hes;
  While others come to spend it, that have grace,
Whilk of thy winnings no labour had nor cure;
  Tak thou example, and spend with merriness;
Without gladness availïs no treasúre.

Though all the wealth that e'er had living wight
  Were only thine, no more thy part does fall
But meat, drink, clothes, and of the rest a sight,

Yet, to the Judge, thou shalt give 'compt of all.
Ane reckoning richt comes of ane ragment small,
Be just and joyous, and do to nane injúre,
    And truth shall mak thee strong, as ony wall;
Without gladness availis no treasuré

WILLIAM DUNBAR (1460-1520?)

Consider what St. Augustine said,
That he sought God within himself,
Settle yourself in solitude, and
You will come upon Him in yourself.

ST. TERESA (1515-82)

Do not scrutinize too closely whether you are doing much or little, ill or well, so long as what you do is not sinful, and that you are heartily seeking to do everything for God. Try as far as you can to do everything well, but when it is done do not think about it; try rather to think of what is to be done next. Go on simply in the Lord's way, and do not torment yourself. We ought to hate our faults, but with a quiet, calm hatred; not pettishly and anxiously. We must learn to look patiently at them, and win through them the grace of self-abnegation and humility. Be constant and courageous, and rejoice that He has given you the will to be wholly his.

ST. FRANCIS DE SALES
From *Spiritual Letters*

PILGRIMAGE

Give me my scallop-shell of quiet,
    My staffe of faith to lean upon,
My scrip of joye—immortal diet—
    My bottle of salvation,
My gown of glory, hope's true gage;—
And thus I take my pilgrimage.

61

Blood must be my body's balmer,
    While my soul, like peaceful palmer,
Traveleth towards the land of heaven;
    Other balm will not be given.
Over the silver mountains,
Where spring the nectar fountains
    There will I kiss
    The bowle of blisse,
And drink my everlasting fill
Upon every milken hill:
    My soul will be a-dry before
    But after that will thirst no more.

                              Sir Walter Raleigh (1552-1618)

He that of such a height hath built his mind
And reared the dwelling of his thoughts so strong,
As neither hope nor fear can shake the frame
Of his resolved powers; nor all the wind
Of vanity or malice pierce to wrong
His settled peace, or to disturb the same:
What a fair seat hath he, from whence he may
The boundless wastes and wilds of man survey!

And with how free an eye doth he look down
Upon those lower regions of turmoil,
Where all the storms of passions mainly beat
On flesh and blood! where honour, power, renown,
Are only gay afflictions, golden toil;
Where greatness stands upon as feeble feet
As frailty doth: and only great doth seem
To little minds who do it so esteem.

He looks upon the mightiest monarch's wars,
But only as on stately robberies;
Where evermore the fortune that prevails

Must be the right: the ill-succeeding mars
The fairest and the best-faced enterprise.
Great pirate Pompey lesser pirates quails;
Justice he sees, as if reduced, still
Conspires with power, whose cause must not be ill.

He sees the face of right t'appear as manifold
As are the passions of uncertain man;
Who puts it in all colours, all attires,
To serve his ends, and makes his courses hold.
He sees that, let deceit work what it can,
Plot and contrive base ways to high desires,
That the all-guiding Providence doth yet
All disappoint and mocks the smoke of wit.

Nor is he moved with all the thunder-cracks
Of tyrant's threats, or with the surly brow
Of power, that proudly sits on others' crimes;
Charged with more crying sins than those he checks.
The storms of sad confusion, that may grow
Up in the present for the coming times,
Appal not him; that hath no side at all,
But of himself, and knows the worst can fall.

SAMUEL DANIEL (1562-1619)
From *The Epistle to the Countess of Cumberland*

What wisdom more, what better life, than pleaseth God
    to send?
What worldly goods, what longer use, than pleaseth God
    to lend?
What better fare, than well content, agreeing with thy
    wealth?
What better guest than trusty friend, in sickness and in
    health?
What better bed than Conscience good, to pass the night
    with sleep?

What better work, than daily care from sin thyself to
keep?

What better thought, than think on God, and daily Him
to serve?

What better gift than to the poor, that ready be to
sterve?

What greater praise of God and man, than mercy for to
show?

Who merciless shall mercy find, than mercy shows to
few?

What worse despair than loth to die, for fear to go to
hell?

What greater faith than trust in God, through Christ in
heaven to dwell?

THOMAS TUSSER (c. 1527-80)
Posies for a Country Bed-Chamber

MADRIGAL

What thing can earthly pleasure give
　　That breeds delight when it is past?
Or who so quietly doth live
　　But storms of care do drown at last?
This is the loan of worldly hire,
The more we have the more desire.
Wherefore I hold him best at ease
That lives content with his estate,
And doth not sail in worldly seas
　　Where Mine and Thine do breed debate:
This noble mind, even in a clown,
Is more than to possess a crown.

RICHARD CARLTON (1601)

SONG

Sweet are the thoughts that savour of content;
  The quiet mind is richer than a crown;
Sweet are the nights in careless slumber spent;
  The poor estate scorns fortune's angry frown:
Such sweet content, such minds, such sleep, such bliss,
Beggars enjoy, where princes oft do miss.
The homely house that harbours quiet rest;
  The cottage that affords no pride nor care;
The mean that 'grees with country music best;
  The sweet consort of mirth and music's fare;
  Obscured life sets down a type of bliss:
  A mind content both crown and kingdom is.

ROBERT GREENE (1560-1592)

MEANS TO ATTAIN A HAPPY LIFE

Martial, the things that do attain
    The happy life be these, I find: —
  The richesse left, not got with pain;
    The fruitful ground; the quiet mind;

The equal friend; no grudge, no strife;
    No change of rule, nor goverance;
  Without disease, the healthful life;
    The household of continuance;

The mean diet, no delicate fare;
    True wisdom join'd with simpleness;
  The night discharged of all care,
    Where wine the wit may not oppress.

The faithful wife, without debate;
    Such sleep as may beguile the night;

65

Contented with thine own estate
 Ne wish for death, ne fear his might.

> HENRY HOWARD, Earl of Surrey
> (1516-1547)

ADAPTATION OF HORACE

The man of life upright,
 Whose guiltless heart is free
From all dishonest deeds,
 Or thought of vanity.

The man whose silent days
 In harmless joys are spent,
Whom hopes cannot delude
 Nor sorrow discontent.

That man needs neither towers
 Nor armour for defence,
Nor secret vaults to fly
 From thunder's violence.

He only can behold
 With unaffrighted eyes
The horrors of the deep
 And terrors of the skies.

Thus scorning all the cares
 That fate or fortune brings,
He makes the heaven his book,
 His wisdom heavenly things.

Good thoughts his only friends,
 His wealth a well-spent age,
The earth his sober inn,
 And quiet pilgrimage.

> Attributed to THOMAS CAMPION
> (1567?-1619)

There is a jewel which no Indian mines
Can buy, no chymic art can counterfeit;
It makes men rich in greatest poverty,
Makes water wine, turns wooden cups to gold,
The homely whistle to sweet music's strain:
    Seldom it comes, to few from heaven sent,
    That much in little, all in naught — Content.

JOHN WILBYE
in *Second Set of Madrigals*

In crystal towers richly set
With glittering gems that shine against the sun,
In regal rooms of jasper and of jet,
Content of mind not always likes to won;
But oftentimes it pleaseth her to stay
In simple cotes enclosed with walls of clay.

WILLIAM BYRD (1611)

    You never enjoy the world aright,
till the sea itself floweth in your veins,
till you are clothed with the heavens, and
crowned with the stars:
and perceive yourself to be the sole heir of the
whole world, and more than so, because men are in it
who are every one sole heirs as well as you.
    Till you can sing and rejoice and delight in
God, as misers do in gold, and Kings in Sceptres,

    · · · · · · · · ·

    Till your spirit filleth the whole world,
and the stars are your jewels; . . .
    you never enjoy the world.

THOMAS TRAHERNE (1636-1743)

CONTENT AND RICH

I dwell in Grace's Court,
    Enrich'd with Virtue's rights;
Faith guides my wit, Love leads my will,
    Hope all my mind delights,

In lowly vales I mount
    To pleasure's highest pitch;
My silly shroud true honour brings,
    My poor estate is rich.

My conscience is my crown,
    Contented thoughts my rest,
My heart is happy in itself,
    My bliss is in my breast.

Enough I reckon wealth,
    A mean the surest lot;
That lies too high for base contempt,
    Too low for envy's plot.

My wishes are but few,
    All easy to fulfill,
I make the limits of my power,
    The bounds unto my will.

I feel no care of coin,
    Well-doing is my wealth;
My mind to me an empire is,
    While Grace affordeth health.

I wrestle not with rage,
    While fury's flame doth burn;
It is in vain to stop the stream
    Until the tide doth turn.

But when the flame is out,
 And ebbing wrath doth end;
I turn a late enlargèd foe,
 Into a quiet friend.

And taught with often proof,
 A tempered calm I find,
To be most solace to itself,
 Best cure for angry mind.

To rise by others' fall,
 I deem a losing gain;
All states with others' ruin built,
 To ruin run amain.

No chance of Fortune's calms
 Can cast my comforts down;
When Fortune smiles, I smile to think
 How quickly she will frown.

And when in froward mood
 She proves an angry foe,
Small gain I found to let her come,
 Less loss to let her go.

Robert Southwell (1562-1594)

MY MIND TO ME A KINGDOM IS

My mind to me a kingdom is,
 Such present joys therein I find,
That it excels all other bliss
 That earth affords or grows by kind:
Though much I want which most would have,
Yet still my mind forbids to crave.

No princely pomp, no wealthy store,
 No force to win the victory,

No wily wit to salve a sore,
    No shape to feed a loving eye;
To none of these I yield as thrall:
For why? My mind doth serve for all.

I see how plenty surfeits oft,
    And hasty climbers soon do fall;
I see that those which are aloft,
    Mishap doth threaten most of all;
They get with toil, they keep with fear;
Such cares my mind could never bear.

Content to live, this is my stay,
    I seek no more than may suffice;
I press to bear no haughty sway;
    Look, what I lack, my mind supplies:
Lo, thus I triumph like a king,
Content with what my mind doth bring.

Some have too much, yet still do crave;
    I little have, and seek no more.
They are but poor, though much they have,
    And I am rich with little store;
They poor, I rich; they beg, I give;
They lack, I leave; they pine, I live.

I laugh not at another's loss;
    I grudge not at another's pain;
No worldly waves my mind can toss;
    My state at one doth still remain:
I fear no foe, I fawn no friend;
I loathe not life, nor dread my end.

Some weigh their pleasure by their lust,
    Their wisdom by their rage of will;

Their treasure is their only trust;
 A cloakéd craft their store of skill:
But all the pleasure that I find
 Is to maintain a quiet mind.

My wealth is health and perfect ease;
 My conscience clear my chief defence;
I neither seek by bribes to please,
 Nor by deceit to breed offence:
Thus do I live; thus will I die;
Would all did so as well as I.

Sir Edward Dyer (1550-1607)

THAT SWEET YOKE

Grow rich in that which never taketh rust:
 Whatever fades, but fading pleasure brings.
Draw in thy beams, and humble all thy might
 To that sweet yoke where lasting freedoms be;
Which breaks the clouds, and opens forth the light;
 That doth both shine, and give us sight to see.

Sir Philip Sidney (1554-86)

A PARADISE

When all is done and said,
 In th' end thus shall you find;
He most of all doth bathe in bliss,
 That hath a quiet mind:
And, clear from worldly cares,
 To deem can be content,
The sweetest time in all his life
 In thinking to be spent.
The body subject is
 To fickle Fortune's power,

And to a million of mishaps
    Is casual every hour:
And Death in time doth change
    It to a clod of clay;
Whenas the mind, which is divine,
    Runs never to decay.
Companion none is like
    Unto the mind alone,
For many have been harm'd by speech,
    Through thinking, few, or none.

        From *A Paradise of Dainty Devices*

Fear oftentimes restraineth words,
    But makes not thoughts to cease;
And he speaks best, that hath the skill
    When for to hold his peace.
Our wealth leaves us at death,
    Our kinsmen at the grave:
But virtues of the mind unto
    The heavens with us have.
Wherefore for virtue's sake,
    I can be well content
The sweetest time in all my life,
    To deem in thinking spent.

        From *A Paradise of Dainty Devices*
        LORD THOMAS VAUX (c. 1510-1556)

A BALLAD OF GOOD COUNSEL

Since through virtue increases dignity,
    And virtue, flower and root, is of noblay,
Of any weal of what estate thou be,
    His steps ensue and dread thou no affray;
    Exile all vice, and follow truth alway;
Luve most thy God, who first thy luve began,
And for each inch He will thee quit a span.

Be not o'er proud in thy prosperity,
   For as it comes, so will it pass away;
Thy time to count is short, thou may'st well see,
   For of green grass soon cometh withered hay.
   Labour in truth while there is light of day.
Trust most in God, for He best guide thee can,
And for an inch He will thee quit a span.

Since word is thrall, and only thought is free,
   Tame thou thy tongue, that power and may,
Shut thou thine eyes on worldly vanity;
   Refrain thy lust and hearken what I say;
   Seize lest thou slide, and creep forth on the way;
Keep thy behest unto thy God and man,
And for each inch He will thee quit a span.

KING JAMES I (1566-1625)

CHARACTER OF A HAPPY LIFE

How happy is he born and taught
   That serveth not another's will;
Whose armour is his honest thought,
   And simple truth his utmost skill!

Whose passions not his masters are,
   Whose soul is still prepared for death,
Untied unto the world by care
   Of public fame or private breath;

Who hath his life from rumors freed,
   Whose conscience is his strong retreat;
Whose state can neither flatterers feed,
   Nor ruin make accusers great;

Who envieth none whom chance doth raise
   Or vice: who never understood

How deepest wounds are given with praise:
    Nor rules of state, but rules of good:

Who God doth late and early pray
    More of his grace than gifts to lend;
Who entertains the harmless day
    With a well-chosen book or friend;

— This man is free from servile bands
    Of hope to rise, or fear to fall;
Lord of himself, though not of lands;
    And having nothing, he hath all.

SIR HENRY WOTTON (1568-1639)

Homely hearts do harbour quiet,
    Little fear and mickle solace;
States suspect their bed and diet;
    Fear and craft do haunt the palace.
    Little would I, little want I,
    When the mind and store agreeth;
Smallest comfort is not scanty;
    Least he longs that little seeth.
    Time hath been that I have longed,
    Foolish and to like of folly.
To converse where honour thronged,
    To my pleasures linked wholly.
    Now I see, and seeing sorrow,
    That the day consum'd returns not;
Who dare trust upon tomorrow,
    When nor time nor life sojourns not.

THOMAS LODGE (1558?-1625)
From *Old Damon's Pastoral*

Man is his own star; and the soul that can
Render an honest and a perfect man
Commands all light, all influence, all fate;

BEAUMONT & FLETCHER
(1584-1616, 1579-1625)

My crown is in my heart, not on my head;
Not deck'd with diamonds and Indian stones,
Nor to be seen: my crown is called content;
A crown it is, that seldom kings enjoy.

SHAKESPEARE (1564-1616)
3 *Henry VI* - III, 1

Ay, but give me worship and quietness;
I like it better than a dangerous honour.

SHAKESPEARE (1564-1616)
Henry I - III

Art thou poor, yet hast thou golden slumbers?
   O, sweet content!
Art thou rich, yet is thy mind perplexéd?
   O punishment!
Dost thou laugh to see how fools are vexéd
To add to golden numbers, golden numbers?
O sweet content, O sweet, O sweet content!
Canst drink the waters of the crispéd spring?
   O sweet content!
Swimm'st thou in wealth, yet sink'st in thine own tears?
   O punishment!
Then he that patiently Want's burden bears
No burden bears, but is a king, a king!
O sweet content! O sweet, O sweet content!
   Work apace, apace, apace, apace;
   Honest labour bears a lovely face;
Then hey nonny nonny, hey nonny nonny!

Content from *Patient Grissel*
THOMAS DEKKER (1570?-1637?)

THE PRAISE OF FORTUNE

Fortune smiles, cry holiday!
   Dimples on her cheek do dwell.
   Fortune frowns, cry well-a-day!
   Her love is heaven, her hate is hell.
Since heaven and hell obey her power, —
Tremble when her eyes do lower.
Since heaven and hell her power obey,
When she smiles, cry holiday!
   Holiday with joy we cry,
   And bend and bend, and merrily
   Sing hymns to Fortune's deity,
   Sing hymns to Fortune's deity.

Chorus

Let us sing merrily, merrily, merrily,
With songs let heaven resound.
Fortune's hands our heads have crowned.
Let us sing merrily, merrily, merrily.

from *Old Fortunatus*
THOMAS DEKKER

When I look before me,
   There I do behold
There's none that sees or knows me;
All the world's a-gadding,
Running madding;
   None doth his station hold.

He that is below envieth his that riseth,
And he that is above, him that's below despiseth,
So every man his plot and counter-plot deviseth.
   Hallo, my fancy, whither wilt thou go?

   Look, look, what bustling
      Here I do espy;

Each another jostling,
Every one turmoiling,
Th'other spoiling,
  As I did pass them by.

One sitteth musing in a dumpish passion,
Another hangs his head because he's out of fashion,
A third is fully bent on sport and recreation.
  Hallo, my fancy, whither wilt thou go?

  Amidst the foamy ocean,
    Fain would I know
  What doth cause the motion,
  And returning
  In its journeying,
    And doth so seldom swerve!

And how these little fishes that swim beneath salt water,
Do never blind their eye; methinks it is a matter
An inch above the reach of old Erra Pater!
  Hallo, my fancy, whither wilt thou go?

  Fain would I be resolved
    How things are done;
  And where the bull was calved
  Of bloody Phalaris,
  And where the tailor is
    That works to the man i' the moon!

Fain would I know how Cupid aims so rightly;
And how these little fairies do dance and leap so lightly;
And where fair Cynthia makes her ambles nightly.
  Hallo, my fancy, whither wilt thou go?

  In conceit like Phaeton,
    I'll mount Phoebus' chair,

77

Having ne'er a hat on,
All my hair a-burning
In my journeying,
    Hurrying through the air.

Fain would I hear his fiery horses neighing,
And see how they on foamy bits are playing:
All the stars and planets I will be surveying!
    Hallo, my fancy, whither wilt thou go? . . .

Hallo, my fancy, hallo,
    Stay, stay at home with me;
I can thee no longer follow,
For thou hast betrayed me,
And bewrayed me;
    It is too much for me.

Stay, stay at home with me; leave off thy lofty soaring;
Stay thou at home with me, and on thy books be poring;
For he that goes abroad, lays little up in storing;
Thou'rt welcome home, my fancy, welcome home to me.

             From *Hallo, my Fancy*
             WILLIAM CLELAND (c. 1661-1689)

As joys are double,
    So is trouble.
Yet even the greatest griefs,
    May be reliefs,
Could we but take them right, and in their ways.
    Happy is he whose heart
    Has found the art
To turn his double pains to double praise.

             GEORGE HERBERT (1593-1632)

GOOD PRECEPTS, OR COUNSEL

In all thy need be thou possesst
Still with a well prepared breast.

Nor let the shackles make thee sad.
Thou canst but have what others had.
And this for comfort thou must know,
Times that are ill won't still be so,
Clouds will not ever pour down rain.
A sullen day will clear again.
First, peals of thunder we must hear,
Then lutes and harps shall stroke the ear.

ROBERT HERRICK (1591-1674)

Content consisteth not in heaping more fuel, but in taking away some fire.

THOMAS FULLER (1608-61)

... But, Master, first let me tell you, that very hour which you were absent from me, I sat down under a willow-tree by the water-side, and considered what you had told me of the owner of that pleasant meadow in which you then left me; that he had a plentiful estate, and not a heart to think so; that he had at this time many lawsuits depending; and that they both damped his mirth, and took up so much of his time and thoughts, that he himself had not leisure to take the sweet content that I, who pretended no little to them, took in his fields: ...

... I say, as I thus sat, joying in my own happy condition, and pitying this poor rich man that owned this and many other pleasant groves and meadows about me, I did thankfully remember what my Saviour said, that the meek possess the earth; or rather, they enjoy what the others possess, and enjoy not; for anglers and meek, quiet-spirited men are free from those high, those restless thoughts, which corrode the sweets of life; and they, and they only, can say, as the poet has happily expresst it—

79

Hail, blest estate of lowliness;
    Happy enjoyments of such minds
As, rich in self-contentedness,
    Can, like the reeds, in roughest winds,
By yielding make that blow but small
At which proud oaks and cedars fall.

ISAAK WALTON (1593-1683)
From *Anglers in the Meadow*

"I knew a man who had health and riches, and several houses all beautiful and ready furnished, and would often trouble himself and family to be removing from one house to another; and being asked by a friend why he removed so often from one house to another, replied, "It was to find content in some one of them." But his friend, knowing his temper, told him, if he would find content in any of his houses, he must leave himself behind him; for content will never dwell but in a meek and quiet soul...."

ISAAK WALTON
in *The Compleat Angler*

Stone walls do not a prison make,
    Nor iron bars a cage;
Minds innocent and quiet take
    That for an hermitage;
If I have freedom in my love,
And in my soul am free,
Angels alone that soar above
    Enjoy such liberty.

RICHARD LOVELACE (1618-1658)
To Althea from prison, IV.

Halt! whither runnest thou? Heaven is in thee: seekest thou God otherwhere, thou missest Him ever and ever.

ANGELINUS SILENIS (1624-1677)

Who governs his own course with steady hand,
Who does himself with sovereign power command;
Whom neither death nor poverty does fright,
Who stands not awkwardly in his own light
Against the truth: who can, when pleasures knock
Loud at his door, keep from the bolt and lock.
Who can, though honour at his gate should stay
In all her masking cloaths, send her away,
And cry 'Begone, I have no mind to play.'

This, I confess, is a freeman . . .

For the few hours of life allotted me,
Give me (great God) but bread and libertie.
I'll beg no more: if more thou'rt pleas'd to give,
I'll thankfully that overplus receive;
If beyond this no more be freely sent,
I'll thank for this, and go away content.

Abraham Cowley (1618-67)
From the Essays *Of Liberty*

This only grant me, that my means may lye
Too low for envy, for contempt too high.
     Some honour I would have,
Not from great deeds, but good alone;
The unknown are better, than ill known:
     Rumour can ope the grave.
Acquaintance I would have, but when 't depends
Not on the number, but the choice of friends.

Books should, not business, entertain the light,
And sleep, as undisturb'd as death, the night.
     My house a cottage more
Than palace; and should fitting be
For all my use, no luxurie

My garden painted o'er
With nature's hand, not arts; and pleasures yield,
Horace might envy in his Sabine field.

Thus would I double my life's fading space;
For he, that runs it well, twice runs his race.
　　And in this true delight,
These unbought sports, that happy state,
I would not fear, nor wish my fate;
　　But boldly say each night,
Tomorrow let my sun his beams display,
Or, in clouds hide them; I have liv'd to-day.

ABRAHAM COWLEY, from *Discourse*

Who sees the heavenly ancient Ways,
　Of GOD the Lord, with Joy and Praise;
　　　More than the Skies,
　　　With open Eyes,
　Doth prize them all: yea more than Gems
　　　And Regal Diadems.
That more esteemeth Mountains as they are,
　　Than if they Gold and Silver were:
　　To whom the SUN more pleasure brings,
Then Crowns and Thrones, and Palaces, to Kings.
　　　That knows his Ways,
　　　To be the Joys,
　And Way of God. These things who knows,
　　With Joy and Praise he goes!

From *The Ways of Wisdom*
or *Thanksgiving for the Beauty of his Providence*
THOMAS TRAHERNE (1634-74)

PARAPHRASE OF HORACE

Happy the man and happy he alone,
　He who can call To-day his own;
　He who secure within can say,

82

To-morrow do thy worst, for I have liv'd to-day;
    Be fair or foul or rain or shine,
    The joys I have possess'd in spite of Fate are mine.
Not Heaven itself upon the Past has Power,
But what has been, has been, and I have had my Hour.
Fortune, that with malicious joy,
    Does Man, her Slave, oppress,
Proud of her office to destroy,
    Is seldom pleas'd to bless.
Still various, and unconstant still,
But with an Inclination to be ill;
Promotes, degrades, delights in Strife,
And makes a lottery of Life.
I can enjoy her while she's kind;
But when she dances in the Wind,
And shakes her wings and will not stay,
I puff the Prostitute away:
The little of the much she gave is quietly resigned.
Content with Poverty, my Soul I arm:
And Virtue, tho in rags, will keep me warm.
                          JOHN DRYDEN (1631-1700)

THE QUIET LIFE

Happy the man, whose wish and care
    A few paternal acres bound,
Content to breathe his native air
                In his own ground.

Whose herds with milk, whose fields with bread,
    Whose flocks supply him with attire;
Whose trees in summer yield him shade,
                In winter fire.

Blest, who can unconcern'dly find
    Hours, days, and years slide soft away

In health of body, peace of mind,
                  Quiet by day,

Sound sleep by night; study and ease
        Together mix'd: sweet recreation,
And innocence, which most does please
                  With meditation.

Thus let me live, unseen, unknown;
        Thus unlamented let me die;
Steal from the world, and not a stone
                Tell where I lie.

                    A. POPE (1688-1744)

I care not, Fortune, what you me deny:
    You cannot rob me of free Nature's grace;
You cannot shut the windows of the sky
    Through which Aurora shows her brightening face;
You cannot bar my constant feet to trace
    The woods and lawns, by living stream, at eve.
Let health my nerves and finer fibres brace,
    And I their toys to the great children leave:
Of fancy, reason, virtue, nought can me bereave.

             JAMES THOMSON (1700-48)
             The Castle of Indolence

From the world of sin and noise
        And hurry I withdraw;
For the small and inward voice
        I wait with humble awe;
Silent am I now and still,
        Dare not in Thy presence move;
To my waiting soul reveal
        The secret of Thy love.

            CHARLES WESLEY (1707-88)

FOR DIVINE STRENGTH

Father, in thy mysterious presence kneeling,
    Fain would our souls feel all thy kindling love;
For we are weak, and need some deep revealing
    Of trust and strength and calmness from above.

Lord, we have wandered forth through doubt and sorrow,
    And thou hast made each step an onward one;
And we will ever trust each unknown morrow—
    Thou wilt sustain us till its work is done.

In the heart's depths a peace serene and holy
    Abides: and when pain seems to have her will,
Or we despair, oh! may that peace rise slowly,
    Stronger than agony, and we be still.

Now, Father—now, in thy dear presence kneeling,
    Our spirits yearn to feel thy kindling love;
Now make us strong—we need thy deep revealing
    Of trust and strength and calmness from above.

                              Samuel Johnson (1709-84)

        Joy and woe are woven fine,
        A clothing for the soul divine:
        Under every grief and pine
        Runs a joy with silken twine
        It is right it should be so:
        Man was made for joy and woe;
        And when this we rightly know
        Safely through the world we go.

                    William Blake (1757-1827)
                    From *Auguries of Innocence*

He who bends to himself a joy,
Does the winged life destroy:

But he who kisses the joy as it flies
Lives in eternity's sunrise.

WILLIAM BLAKE (1757-1827)
From *Opportunity*

SONNET LX—THE EVERLASTING TEMPLE

In my mind's eye a Temple, like a cloud
Slowly surmounting some invidious hill,
Rose out of darkness: the bright Work stood still,
And might of its own beauty have been proud,
But it was fashioned and to God was vowed
By Virtues that diffused, in every part,
Spirit divine through forms of human art:
Faith had her arch—her arch, when winds blow loud,
Into the consciousness of safety thrilled;
And Love her towers of dread foundation laid
Under the grave of things; Hope had her spire
Star-high, and pointing still to something higher,
Trembling I gazed, but heard a voice—it said:
"Hell-gates are powerless Phantoms when *we* build."

WILLIAM WORDSWORTH (1770-1850)

. . . One passage in your Letter a little displeas'd me.
The rest was nothing but kindness, which Robert's letters
are ever brimful of. You say that "this World to you
seems drain'd of all its sweets." At first I had hoped you
only meant to intimate the high price of sugar! But I
am afraid you meant more. O Robert, I don't know
what you call sweet. Honey and the honeycomb, roses
and violets, are yet in the earth. The sun and moon yet
reign in Heaven, and the lesser lights keep up their
pretty twinklings. Meats and drinks, sweet sights and
sweet smells, a country walk, spring and autumn, follies
and repentance, quarrels and reconcilements, have all a
sweetness by turns. Good humour and good nature,

friends at home that love you, and friends abroad that miss you—you possess all these things, and more innumerable, and these are all sweet things. You may extract honey from everything. . . .

CHARLES LAMB (1775-1834)
From a Letter to Robert Lloyd, Nov. 13, 1798

RESIGNATION

Why, why repine, my pensive friend,
    At pleasures slipped away?
Some the stern Fates will never lend,
    And all refuse to stay.

I see the rainbow in the sky,
    The dew upon the grass;
I see them, and I ask not why
    They glimmer or they pass.

With folded arms I linger not
    To call them back 'twere vain:
In this, or in some other spot,
    I know they'll shine again.

WALTER SAVAGE LANDOR (1775-1864)

. . . His happiness however, sprung from within himself, and was independent of external circumstances; for he had that inexhaustible good-nature, which is the most precious gift of Heaven; spreading itself like oil over the troubled sea of thought, and keeping the mind smooth and equable in the roughest weather.

WASHINGTON IRVING (1783-1859)
From *The Sketch Book*

I have a bit of Fiat in my soul,
And can myself create my little world.

From *Poems*
THOMAS LOVELL BEDDOES (1803-49)

87

Confide ye aye in Providence,
   For Providence is kind;
An' bear ye a' life's changes
   Wi' a calm and tranquil mind.
Though pressed and hemmed on every side,
   Ha'e faith, an' ye'll win through;
     For ilka blade o' grass
      Keeps its ain drap o' dew.

From *Its ain drap o' Dew*
JAMES BALLANTINE (1808-77)

Open our eyes, Thou Sun of life and gladness, that we may see that glorious world of Thine. It shines for us in vain while drooping sadness enfolds us here like mist: Come Power benign, touch our chill'd hearts with vernal smile, our wintry course do Thou beguile, nor by the wayside ruins let us mourn, who have the eternal towers for our appointed bourne.

JOHN KEBLE (1792-1866)
A Little Prayer at Sunset

SAY NOT,
THE STRUGGLE NAUGHT AVAILETH

Say not, the struggle naught availeth,
   The labour and the wounds are vain,
The enemy faints not, nor faileth,
   And as things have been they remain.

If hopes were dupes, fears may be liars;
   It may be, in yon smoke concealed,
Your comrades chase e'en now the fliers,
   And, but for you, possess the field.

For while the tired waves, vainly breaking,
   Seem here no painful inch to gain,

ADVENTURES IN TRANQUILLITY

Far back, through creeks and inlets making,
　　Comes silent, flooding in, the main.

And not by eastern windows only,
　　When daylight comes, comes in the light;
In front, the sun climbs slow, how slowly,
　　But westward, look, the land is bright.

　　　　　　ARTHUR HUGH CLOUGH (1819-61)

IT FORTIFIES MY SOUL TO KNOW

It fortifies my soul to know
　　That though I perish, Truth is so;
　　That howsoe'er I stray and range,
Whate'er I do, Thou dost not change;
I steadier step when I recall
That if I slip, Thou dost not fall!

　　　　　　ARTHUR HUGH CLOUGH (1819-61)

. . . how many, I say, have found their last peace and comfort in the contemplation of the order of the world, whether manifested in the unvarying movement of the stars, or revealed in the unvarying number of the petals and stamens and pistils of the smallest forget-me-not. How many have felt that to belong to this cosmos, to this beautiful order of nature, is something at least to rest on, something to trust, something to believe, when everything else has failed.

F. MAX MULLER (1823-1900)
in a Hibbert Lecture
See *Life and Religion,* Doubleday, Page 1905

CONTENT

Be it not mine to steal the cultured flower,
　　From any garden of the rich and great,
Nor seek with care through many a weary hour
　　Some novel form of wonder to create.

ADVENTURES IN TRANQUILLITY

Enough for me the leafy woods to rove,
    And gather simple cups of morning dew,
Or in the fields and meadows that I love
    Find beauty in their bells of every hue.
Thus round my cottage floats a fragrant air
    And though the rustic plot be humbly laid,
Yet, like the lilies gladly growing there,
    I have not toiled . . .
My Lord Ambition passed, and smiled in scorn:
I plucked a rose, and, lo! it had no thorn.

GEORGE JOHN ROMANES (1848-94)

THE THINGS I MISS

An easy thing, O Power Divine,
To thank thee for these gifts of mine!
    For summer's sunshine, winter's snow,
For hearts that kindle, thoughts that glow.
But when shall I attain to this,—
To thank thee for the things I miss?
For all young Fancy's early gleams,
The dreamed-of joys that still are dreams,
Hopes unfulfilled, and pleasures known
Through others' fortunes, not my own,
And blessings seen that are not given,
And never will be, this side heaven.
Had I too shared the joys I see,
Would there have been a heaven for me?
Could I have felt thy presence near,
Had I possessed what I held dear?
My deepest fortune, highest bliss,
Have grown perchance from things I miss.
Sometimes there comes an hour of calm;
Grief turns to blessing, pain to balm;

A Power that works above my will
Still leads me onward, upward still:
And then my heart attains to this—
To thank thee for the things I miss.

Thomas Wentworth Higginson (1823-1911)

SELF-DEPENDENCE

Weary of myself, and sick of asking
    What I am, and what I ought to be,
At this vessel's prow I stand, which bears me
    Forwards, forwards, o'er the starlit sea.

And a look of passionate desire
    O'er the sea and to the stars I send:
"Ye who from my childhood up have calmed me,
    Calm me, ah, compose me to the end!

Ah, once more," I cried, "ye stars, ye waters,
    On my heart your mighty charm renew;
Still, still let me, as I gaze upon you,
    Feel my soul becoming vast like you."

From the intense, clear, star-sown vault of heaven,
    Over the lit sea's unquiet way,
In the rustling night-air came the answer:—
    "Wouldst thou *be* as these are? *Live* as they.

"Unaffrighted by the silence round them,
    Undistracted by the sights they see,
These demand not that the things without them
    Yield them love, amusement, sympathy.

"And with joy the stars perform their shining,
    And the sea its long moon-silvered roll;
For self-poised they live, nor pine with noting
    All the fever of some differing soul.

"Bounded by themselves, and unregardful
    In what state God's other works may be,
In their own tasks all their powers pouring,
    These attain the mighty life you see."

O air-born voice! long since, severely clear,
    A cry like thine in mine own heart I hear:—
"Resolve to be thyself; and know that he
    Who finds himself, loses his misery!"

                    MATTHEW ARNOLD (1822-88)

QUIET WORK

One lesson, Nature, let me learn of thee,
One lesson which in every wind is blown,
One lesson of two duties kept at one
Though the loud world proclaim their enmity—
Of toil unsever'd from tranquillity!
Of labour, that in lasting fruit outgrows
Far noisier schemes, accomplish'd in repose,
Too great for haste, too high for rivalry!
Yes, while on earth a thousand discords ring,
Man's senseless uproar mingling with his toil,
Still do thy quiet ministers move on,
Their glorious tasks in silence perfecting;
Still working, blaming still our vain turmoil;
Labourers that shall not fail, when man is gone.

                    MATTHEW ARNOLD (1822-88)

To live content with small means; to seek elegance
rather than luxury, and refinement rather than fashion;
to be worthy, not respectable; and wealthy, not rich; to
study hard, think quietly, talk gently, act frankly; to listen to stars and birds, babes and sages, with open heart;
to bear all cheerfully, do all bravely, await occasions,
hurry never; in a word, to let the spiritual, unbidden and

unconscious, grow up through the common. This is to be my symphony.

From *My Symphony*
WILLIAM HENRY CHANNING (1780-1842)

COMPENSATION

The wings of time are black and white,
Pied with morning and with night.
Mountain tall and ocean deep
Trembling balance duly keep.
In changing moon and tidal wave
Glows the feud of Want and Have.
Gauge of more and less through space,
Electric star or pencil plays,
The lonely earth amid the balls
That hurry through the eternal halls,
A makeweight flying to the void,
Supplemental asteroid,
Or compensatory spark,
Shoots across the neutral Dark.

Man's the elm, and Wealth the vine;
Stanch and strong the tendrils twine:
Though the frail ringlets thee deceive,
None from its stock that vine can reave.
Fear not, then, thou child infirm,
There's no god dare wrong a worm;
Laurel crowns cleave to deserts,
And power to him who power exerts.
Hast not thy share? On winged feet,
Lo! it rushes thee to meet;
And all that Nature made thy own,
Floating in air or pent in stone,

Will rive the hills and swim the seas
And, like thy shadow, follow thee.

RALPH WALDO EMERSON
Houghton Mifflin Company

  ". . . I am she
  Whom the gods love, Tranquillity;
Who wins me late, but keeps me long,
Who, dowered with every gift of passion,
In that fierce flame can forge and fashion
    Of sin and self the anchor strong;
Can thence compel the driving force
Of daily life's mechanic course,
Nor less the nobler energies
Of needful toil and culture wise;
Whose soul is worth the tempter's lure,
Who can renounce and yet endure,
To him I come, not lightly wooed,
    But won by silent fortitude."

From *Ode to Happiness*
JAMES RUSSELL LOWELL (1819-91)
Houghton Mifflin Company

My faith is larger than the hills,
So when the hills decay,
My faith must take the purple wheel
To show the Sun the way.
'Tis first he steps upon the vane
And then upon the hill;
And then abroad the world he goes
To do his golden will.
And if his yellow feet should miss,
The birds would not arise,
The flowers would slumber on their stems,—
No bells have Paradise.

How dare I therefore stint a faith
On which so vast depends,
Lest Firmament should fail for me—
The rivet in the bands.

EMILY DICKINSON (1830-86)

It is well to find your employment and amusement in simple and homely things. These wear best and yield most. I think I would rather watch the motions of these cows in their pastures for a day, which I now see all headed one way and slowly advancing, watch them and project their course carefully on a chart, and report all their behavior faithfully, than wander to Europe or Asia, and watch other motions there; for it is only ourselves that we report in either case, and perchance we shall report a more restless, worthless self in the latter case than in the former.

HENRY DAVID THOREAU (1817-62)
From *Autumn,* Oct. 5, 1856
Houghton Mifflin Company

Life is grand and so are its environments of Past and Future. Would the face of nature be so serene and beautiful if man's destiny were not equally so?

THOREAU
From *Early Spring*

A man must invest himself near at hand and in common things, and be content with a steady and moderate return, if he would know the blessedness of a cheerful heart, and the sweetness of a walk over the round earth.

JOHN BURROUGHS (1837-1921)
Houghton Mifflin Company

WAITING

Serene I fold my hands and wait,
    Nor care for wind, nor tide, nor sea;

I rave no more 'gainst time or fate,
    For, lo! my own shall come to me.

I stay my haste, I make delays,
    For what avails this eager pace?
I stand amid the eternal ways,
    And what is mine shall know my face.

Asleep, awake, by night or day,
    The friends I seek are seeking me;
No wind can drive my bark astray,
    Nor change the tide of destiny.

What matter if I stand alone?
    I wait with joy the coming years;
My heart shall reap where it hath sown,
    And garner up its fruit of tears.

The waters know their own and draw
    The brook that springs in yonder heights;
So flows the good with equal law
    Unto the soul of pure delights.

The stars come nightly to the sky;
    The tidal wave comes to the sea;
Nor time, nor space, nor deep, nor high,
    Can keep my own away from me.

Houghton Mifflin Company
JOHN BURROUGHS (1837-1921)

FOR JOY

For each and every joyful thing
For twilight swallows on the wing,
For all that nest and all that sing,—

For fountains cool that laugh and leap,
For rivers running to the deep,
For happy, care-forgetting sleep,—

For stars that pierce the sombre dark,
For morn, awaking with the lark,
For life new-stirring 'neath the bark,—

For sunshine and the blessed rain,
For budding grove and blossomy lane,
For the sweet silence of the plain,—

For bounty springing from the sod,
For every step by beauty trod.—
For each dear gift of joy, thank God!

FLORENCE EARLE COATES (1850-1927)
The Unconquered Air and Other Poems
1912
Houghton Mifflin Company

WHEN THOUGHT LIES BEAUTIFUL AND KIND

When thought lies beautiful and kind
In the still places of the mind,
There is a woodland one may find.

The sheen of birch, on green of fir,
In that deep grove is lovelier
Than bells of silver set astir.

The wild rose blooms without a thorn.
The slender cream-white unicorn
Lifts the whorled amber of his horn.

On hooves of bronze he goes unshod.
Sprung from each cup his foot has trod
A ring of violets flowers the sod,

Yellow and white and purple-blue.
None save the visionary few
May trace those clusters in the dew.

One must be natural as a tree,
One must be water-clear to see
That rippling flank of ivory.

None may beguile him, none may ride;
But he whose heart is still and wide
Draws near the wonder of his side.

And he who dreams not to profane
That beauteous shoulder with the rein
Shall walk with fingers in his mane!

ELEANOR BALDWIN
in *The Christian Science Monitor*
April 10, 1936

THE HAPPIEST HEART

Who drives the horses of the sun
Shall lord it but a day;
Better the lowly deed were done,
And kept the humble way.
The rust will find the sword of fame,
The dust will hide the crown;
Ay, none shall nail so high his name
Time will not tear it down.
The happiest heart that ever beat
Was in some quiet breast
That found the common daylight sweet,
And left to Heaven the rest

JOHN VANCE CHENEY (1848-1922)

But what was before us we know not,
And we know not what shall succeed.
    Haply, the river of Time—
As it grows, as the towns on its marge
Fling their wavering lights
On a wider, statelier stream—
May acquire, if not the calm
Of its earlier mountainous shore,
Yet a solemn peace of its own.

And the width of the waters, the hush
Of the grey expanse where he floats,
Freshening its current and spotted with foam
As it draws to the Ocean, may strike
Peace to the soul of the man on its breast—
As the pale waste widens around him,
As the banks fade dimmer away,
As the stars come out, and the night-wind
Brings up the stream
Murmurs and scents of the infinite sea.

Concluding stanzas of *The Future*
MATTHEW ARNOLD

Some persons, I know, estimate happiness by fine houses, gardens, and parks—others by pictures, horses, money, and various things wholly remote from their own species; but when I wish to ascertain the real felicity of any rational man, I always inquire *whom has he to love?* If I find he has nobody, or does not love those he has— even in the midst of all his profusion of finery and grandeur, I pronounce him a being deep in adversity.

MRS. INCHBALD
From *Nature and Art,* pub. in 1796

SONG

Let my voice ring out and over the earth,
    Through all the grief and strife,
With a golden joy in a silver mirth:
    Thank God for life!

Let my voice swell out through the great abyss,
    To the azure dome above,
With a chord of faith in the harp of bliss:
    Thank God for Love!

Let my voice thrill out beneath and above,
　　The whole world through:
O my Love and Life, O my Life and Love,
　　Thank God for you!

JAMES THOMSON (1700-48)

TRANQUILLITY

Weary, and marred with care and pain
And bruising days, the human brain
Draws wounded inward,—it might be
Some delicate creature of the sea,
That, shuddering, shrinks its lucent dome,
And coils its azure tendrils home,
And folds its filmy curtains tight
At jarring contact, e'er so light;
But let it float away all free,
And feel the buoyant, supple sea
Among its tinted streamers swell,
Again it spreads its gauzy wings,
And, waving its wan fringes, swings
With rhythmic pulse its crystal bell.
　　　So let the mind, with care o'erwrought,
Float down the tranquil tides of thought:
Calm visions of unending years
Beyond this little moment's fears;
Of boundless regions far from where
The girdle of the azure air
Binds to the earth the prisoned mind.
Set free the fancy, till it find
Beyond our world a vaster place
To thrill and vibrate out through space,—
As some auroral banner streams
Up through the night in pulsing gleams,
And floats and flashes o'er our dreams;

There let the whirling planet fall
Down—down, till but a glimmering ball,
A misty star: and dwindled so,
There is no room for care, or woe,
Or wish, apart from that one Will
That doth the worlds with music fill.

EDWARD ROWLAND SILL (1841-87)
in *Poems*
Houghton Mifflin Company
Copyright 1887

RICHES

What to a man who loves the air
Are trinkets, gauds, and jewels rare?
And what is wealth or fame to one
Who is a brother to the sun;
Who drinks the wine that morning spills
Upon the heaven-kissing hills,
And sees a ray of hope afar
In every glimmer of a star?

What to a man whose god is truth
Are spoils and stratagems, forsooth—
Who looks beyond the doors of death
For loftier life, sublimer breath;
Who can forswear the state of kings
In knowledge of diviner things,
The dreams immortal that unroll
And burst to blossoms in his soul?

ROBERT LOVEMAN
(1864-1923)

SERENITY

With how much care and fret and useless trouble
  We build our souls of unsubstantial things,
Until our minds grow ill, our bodies double!

For lacking wisdom, all our striving brings
    Serenity no nearer. And the springs
Of joy we might have found are choked with stubble.
About our foolish roofless walls of rubble
    Doubts brush, like bats, our faces with their wings.
We have not learned that ancient pagan calm
    With which men, firm in courage, met despair;
Nor peace, which is the Christian's secret charm;
    Nor Nature's deep serenity; the air
Of starlit evening, and a quiet river,
And Death a wind to cool the hottest fever.

THEODORE MAYNARD in G. K.'s Weekly

THE SECRET PACT

My memory hath a secret pact
    Wherein I store the loveliest things;
And in my heart, not on my back,
    My dear and guarded treasure swings.

With every passing year it grows
    And as it grows life fairer gleams;
And lesser weigh my daily woes,
    And brighter, rarer shine my dreams.

My memory hath a secret pact,
    When I am sad I open it
And soon of solace have no lack.
    And all my heart with joy is lit;

And over land, and over sea,
    My thought flies swifter than a dove,
For are not those who smiled on me
    Still keeping bright the lamp of love?

SAMUEL MINTURN
Clipt from an old magazine,
date unidentified.

THESE THINGS SHALL TEACH

These things shall teach man quietude
And loftiness of soul:
The sunlit beach beyond whose edge
Far going waters roll.

The redwood whose old shaggy crest
Has weathered storm and time
And sings a quiet monody
To match the light wind's rhyme.

The mountain's brow unchanged and high
Above a valley changed,
The still horizon's purple deeps
Where ancient hills are ranged.

The scarlet poppy, brief and young,
With deathless Life elate,
The rain-swept meadow's fragrant hush,
With cattle at its gate.

The joyous stream whose tireless course
Unfurls a silver scroll:
All these shall teach man quietude
And loftiness of soul

MAUDE DEVERSE NEWTON
in *The Christian Science Monitor,* 1934

THE COMFORT OF THE STARS

When I am overmatched by petty cares
   And things of earth loom large, and look to be
   Of moment, how it soothes and comforts me
To step into the night and feel the airs

Of heaven fan my cheek; and, best of all,
    Gaze up into those all-uncharted seas
    Where swim the stately planets: such as these
Make mortal fret seem light and temporal.

I muse on what of Life may stir among
    Those spaces knowing naught of metes or bars;
    Undreamed-of dramas played in outmost stars,
And lyrics by archangels grandly sung.

I grow familiar with the solar runes
    And comprehend of worlds the mystic birth:
    Ringed Saturn, Mars, whose fashion apes the earth,
And Jupiter, the giant, with his moons.

Then, dizzy with the unspeakable sights above,
    Rebuked by Vast on Vast, my puny heart
    Is greatened for its transitory part,
My trouble merged in wonder and in love.

RICHARD BURTON
from *Dumb in June*
Lothrop Lee & Shepherd Co.
1896

TRANQUILLITY

O fevered eyes, with searching strained
    Till both the parching globes are pained,
At set of sun is balm for you;
Look up, and bathe them in the blue.
No need to count the coming stars,
Nor watch those wimpled pearly bars
That flush above the west; but follow
In idler mood the idle swallow,
With careless, half-unconscious eye,
Round his great circles on the sky,

Till he, and all things lose for you
Their being in that depth of blue.
O fevered brain, with searching strained
    Till every pulsing nerve is pained,
In tranquil hours is balm for you;
Vex not the thoughts with false and true;
Be still and bathe them in the blue.
To every sad conviction throw
This grim defiance: "Be it so!"
To doubts that will not let you sleep,
This answer: "Wait! the truth will keep!"
With every rising of the sun
Think of your life as just begun.
The past has shrived and buried deep
All yesterdays; there let them sleep.
Nor seek to summon back one ghost
Of that innumerable host
Concern yourself with but today,
Woo it and teach it to obey
Your will and wish. Since time began
Today has been the friend of man,
But in his blindness and his sorrow
He looks to yesterday and tomorrow.
You and today, a soul sublime,
And the great pregnant hour of time
With God himself to bind the twain,
"Go forth," I say, "Attain! Attain!"

Author unidentified

MIRACLE

Who is in love with loveliness
    Need not shake with cold;
For he may tear a star in two,
    And frock himself in gold.

Who holds her first within his heart,
    In certain favor goes;
If his roof tumbles, he may find
    Harbor in a rose.

LIZETTE W. REESE (1856-1935)
Rinehart & Company

WHO WALKS WITH BEAUTY

Who walks with Beauty has no need of fear;
The sun and moon and stars keep pace with him,
Invisible hands restore the ruined year,
And time, itself, grows beautifully dim.
One hill will keep the footprints of the moon,
That came and went a hushed and secret hour;
One star at dusk will yield the lasting boon;
Remembered Beauty's white, immortal flower.
Who takes of Beauty wine and daily bread,
Will know no lack when bitter years are lean;
The brimming cup is by, the feast is spread,—
The sun and moon and stars his eyes have seen,
Are for his hunger and the thirst he slakes:
The wine of Beauty and the bread he breaks.

DAVID MORTON (1886-   )

SONNET III

O world, thou choosest not the better part!
It is not wisdom to be only wise,
And on the inner vision close the eye,
But it is wisdom to believe the heart
Columbus found a world, and had no chart,
Save one that faith deciphered in the skies;
To trust the soul's invincible surmise
Was all his science and his only art.

Our knowledge is a torch of smoky pine
That lights the pathway but one step ahead,
Across a void of mystery and dread.
Bid, then, the tender light of faith to shine,
By which alone the mortal heart is led
Unto the thinking of the thought divine.

> GEORGE SANTAYANA (1863-1953)
> in *Sonnets and Other Verses,* 1906
> Duffield & Company

CERTAINTY

Not for one single day
Can I discern my way
But this I surely know,—
Who gives the day,
Will shew the way,
    So I securely go.

> JOHN OXENHAM (185?-1941)

FAITH

What are we bound for? What's the yield
    Of all this energy and waste?
Why do we spend ourselves and build
    With such an empty haste?
Wherefore the bravery we boast?
    How can we spend one laughing breath
When at the end all things are lost
    In ignorance and death?
The stars have found a blazing course
    In a vast curve that cuts through space;
Enough for us to feel that force
    Swinging us through the days.

Enough that we have strength to sing
    And fight and somehow scorn the grave;
That life's too bold and bright a thing
    To question or to save.

> LOUIS UNTERMEYER
> from *Selected Poems and Parodies of
> Louis Untermeyer*

PANDORA'S SONG

Of wounds and sore defeat
I made my battle stay;
Wingéd sandals for my feet
I wove of my delay;
Of weariness and fear,
I made my shouting spear;
Of loss, and doubt, and dread,
And swift oncoming doom
I made a helmet for my head
And a floating plume
From the strutting mist of death,
And the failure of the breath,
I made a battle-horn to blow
Across the vales of overthrow.
O hearken, love, the battle-horn!
The triumph clear, the silver scorn!
O hearken where the echoes bring,
Down the grey disastrous morn,
Laughter and rallying!

> WILLIAM VAUGHN MOODY (1869-1910)
> Houghton Mifflin Company

HE WHOM A DREAM HATH POSSESSED

He whom a dream hath possessed knoweth no more of
    doubting,

For mist and the blowing of winds and the mouthing of
    words he scorns;
Not the sinuous speech of schools he hears, but a knightly
    shouting,
And never comes darkness down, yet he greeteth a mil-
    lion morns.
He whom a dream hath possessed knoweth no more of
    roaming;
All roads and the flowing of waves and the speediest
    flight he knows,
But wherever his feet are set, his soul is forever homing,
And going he comes, and coming he heareth a call and
    goes.
He whom a dream hath possessed knoweth no more of
    sorrow,
At death and the dropping of leaves and the fading of
    suns he smiles,
For a dream remembers no past and scorns the desire of
    a morrow,
And a dream in a sea of doom sets surely the ultimate
    isles.
He whom a dream hath possessed treads the impalpable
    marches,
From the dust of the day's long road he leaps to a laugh-
    ing star,
And the ruin of worlds that fall he views from eternal
    arches,
And rides God's battlefield in a flashing and golden car.

SHAEMAS O' SHEEL (1886-   )

FIRST GREEN OF SPRING

This green has only one meaning,
It is foreign to despair.

ADVENTURES IN TRANQUILLITY

The earth knows nothing of uncertainty,
It has felt the sun-warmed air.
The bird has not faltered on the bough,
Nor has the seed delayed—
Wondering if this leaf were worth making—
Or that new grass blade.

ELIZABETH COATSWORTH
in *The Christian Science Monitor,*
June 11, 1942.

THE MOSS

When black despair beats down my wings,
    And heavenly visions fade away—
Lord, let me bend to common things,
    The tasks of every day;
As, when th' aurora is denied
    And blinding blizzards round him beat,
The Samoyad stoops, and takes for guide
    The moss beneath his feet.

WILLIAM CANTON (1845-1926)
From *W. V. Her Book and Various Verses*
Stone & Kimball, 1897

THE WANDERER

He knows no home; he only knows
    Hunger and cold and pain.
The four winds are his bedfellows;
    His sleep is dashed with rain.
'Tis naught to him who fails, who thrives:
    He neither hopes nor fears;
Some dim primeval impulse drives
    His footsteps down the years.
He could not, if he would, forsake
    Lone road and field and tree.

Yet think! it takes a God to make
 E'en such a waif as he.
And once a maiden, asked for bread,
 Saw, as she gave her dole,
No friendless vagrant, but instead,
 An indefeasible Soul.

WILLIAM CANTON (1845-1926)
from *W. V. Her Book and Various Verses*
Stone & Kimball, 1897

Trust in thyself,—then spur amain!
 So shall Charybdis wear a grace,
Grim Aetna laugh, the Libyan plain
 Take roses to her shrivelled face.
  This orb—this round
  Of sight and sound—
Count it the lists that God hath built
For haughty hearts to ride a-tilt.

ARTHUR QUILLER-COUCH
From *The Splendid Spur*

COURAGE

Courage is but a word, and yet, of words,
The only sentinel of permanence;
The ruddy watch-fire of cold winter days,
We steal its comfort, lift our weary swords,
And on. For faith—without it—has no sense;
And love to wind of doubt and tremor sways;
And life for ever quaking marsh must tread.
Laws give it not, before it prayer will blush,
Hope has it not, nor pride of being true.
'Tis the mysterious soul which never yields,
But hales us on and on to breast the rush
Of all the fortunes we shall happen through.

And when Death calls across his shadowy fields—
Dying, it answers: "Here! I am not dead!"
JOHN GALSWORTHY (1867-1933)
in Moods, Songs and Doggerels
Charles Scribner's Sons, 1912.

Plant patience in the garden of thy soul,
The roots are bitter, but the fruit is sweet,
And when at last it stands complete
Beneath the tender shade, the burning heat and
   burdens of the day shall lose control
Plant patience in the garden of thy soul.
Author unidentified

MAKE FRIENDS WITH QUIET

Make friends with quiet when the day is leaving,
Slacken your heart's pace.
Take time and notice the sky's way of wearing
Old stars in a new place.
Let stillness hold your hands, tell you a story
Folding those chattering birds—
Spoken in clover or twined out in script
Of honeysuckle words.
If silence loves you, you may hear a secret
Dropped from a linden tower,
The three notes the catbird says for memory
In the lilac-colored hour.
YETZA GILLESPIE
in The Christian Science Monitor,
August 8, 1941

GLADNESS

The world has brought not anything
   To make me glad to-day!
The swallow had a broken wing

And after all my journeying
There was no water in the spring—
    My friend has said me nay,
But yet somehow I needs must sing
    As on a luckier day.

Dusk falls as gray as any tear,
    There is no hope in sight!
But something in me seems so fair,
That like a star I needs must wear!
A safety made of shining air
Between me and the night.
Such inner weavings do I wear
    All fashioned of delight.

I need not for these robes of mine
    The loveliness of earth,
But happenings remote and fine
Like threads of dreams will blow and shine
In gossamer and crystalline,
And I was glad from birth.
So even while my eyes repine
    My heart is clothed in mirth.

              ANNA HEMPSTEAD BRANCH (1875-1937)
              H. Mifflin
              Houghton Mifflin Company
              from *The Shoes That Danced and Other Poems,* 1895.

IMMANENCE

My thoughts go out like spider-threads,
    Cast forth upon the air;
Filmy and fine, and floating wide,
    Caught by whatever may betide
To seek thee everywhere.

ADVENTURES IN TRANQUILLITY

In league with every breeze that blows
    All ways, all holds they dare;
North, east, or south, or west they fly,
    And sure, though winds be low or high,
To find thee everywhere.

Love still is lord of space and fate:
    All roads his runners fare;
All heights that bar, they laughing climb;
    They find all days the fitting time,
And highways everywhere.

Author unidentified

TO THE MODERN MAN

From mysteries of the Past
    The Future is prophesied.
The Actual comes and goes
    Like shadows on a tide.

Realities come and go
    Like shadows on a pool,—
The leaves are for the wise man,
    The shadow for the fool.

Out of the moment Now
    Rises the god To-Be,
The light upon his brow
    Is from eternity

Leave dreaming to the fool
    And take things as they are;
All things are in yourself,
    Who stand upon a star

And look upon the stars
    And yearn with deepening breath—

114

All things are in yourself—
　　Love and Life and Death.

JOHN HALL WHEELOCK (1886-　　)
from *The Beloved Adventure*

THREE COUNSELLORS

It was the fairy of the place,
Moving within a little light,
Who touched with dim and shadowy grace
The conflict at its fever height.
It seemed to whisper "Quietness",
Then quietly itself was gone:
Yet echoes of its mute caress
Were with me as the years went on.
It was the warrior within
Who called "Awake, prepare for fight:
Yet lose not memory in the din:
Make of thy gentleness thy might:
"Make of thy silence words to shake
The long-enthroned kings of earth:
Make of thy will the force to break
Their towers of wantonness and mirth."
It was the wise, all-seeing soul
Who counselled neither war nor peace:
"Only be thou thyself that goal
In which the wars of time shall cease."

A. E. (GEORGE RUSSELL) (1867-1935)
from *Selected Poems by A. E.*
Macmillan Company, 1935.

END WORD

To suffer woes which Hope thinks infinite;
To forgive wrongs darker than death or night;

To defy Power, which seems omnipotent;
To love, and bear; to hope till Hope creates
From its own wreck the thing it contemplates;
　　Neither to change, nor falter, nor repent;
This, like thy glory, Titan, is to be
Good, great and joyous, beautiful and free;
This is alone Life, Joy, Empire, and Victory.

PERCY BYSSHE SHELLEY (1792-1822)
Concluding stanza, *Prometheus Unbound*

INDEX OF AUTHORS QUOTED FOR THE ANTHOLOGY

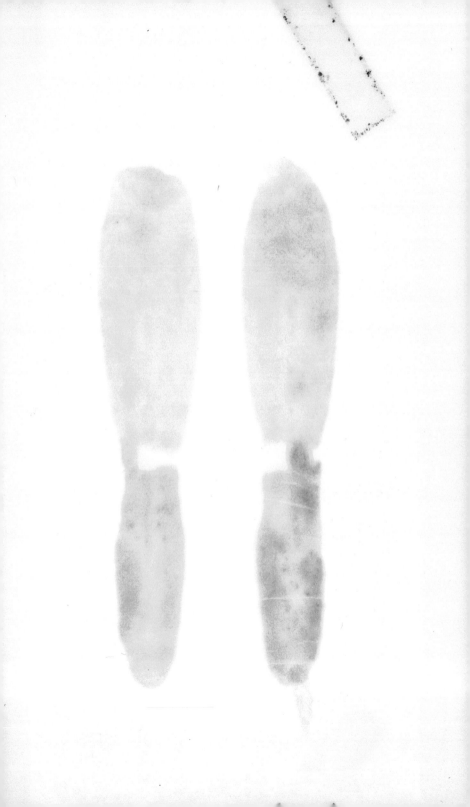

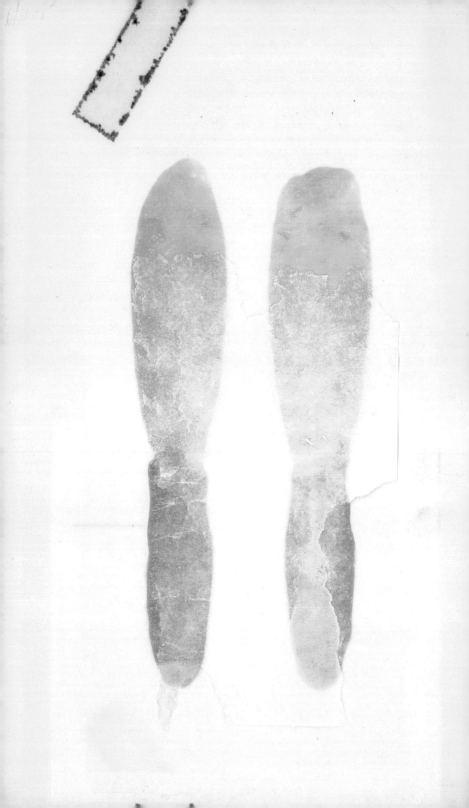